CRITICAL
ANTHOLOGIES OF
NONFICTION
WRITING™

CRITICAL PERSPECTIVES ON
WORLD WAR II

Edited by
JAMES W. FISCUS

THE ROSEN PUBLISHING GROUP, INC.
NEW YORK

Published in 2005 by The Rosen Publishing Group, Inc.
29 East 21st Street, New York, NY 10010

Library of Congress Cataloging-in-Publication Data

Critical perspectives on World War II / edited by James W. Fiscus.—1st ed.
    p. cm.—(Critical anthologies of nonfiction writing)
Includes bibliographical references and index.
ISBN 1-4042-0065-7 (library binding)
1. World War, 1939–1945—Sources. I. Fiscus, James W.
II. Series.
D743.C75 2004
940.53—dc22

                    2004001592

Manufactured in the United States of America

On the cover: Left to right: British prime minister Winston S. Churchill, U.S. president Franklin D. Roosevelt, and Soviet leader Joseph Stalin meet at the Yalta Conference in February, 1945.

CONTENTS

Introduction 4

CHAPTER ONE Time, Continuity, and Change:
STORM CLOUDS OF WAR 11

CHAPTER TWO People, Places, and Environments:
WORLD REACTION TO WORLD WAR 44

CHAPTER THREE Power, Authority, and Governance:
HATE AND PATRIOTISM 76

CHAPTER FOUR Individuals, Groups, and Institutions:
PEOPLE IN WAR 98

CHAPTER FIVE Global Connections:
THE THEATERS OF WAR 130

Timeline 162
For More Information 164
For Further Reading 164
Annotated Bibliography 166
Index 172

INTRODUCTION

he 100 years of the twentieth century will be remembered for the best and the worst humanity can produce. It will be remembered for magnificent accomplishments in art, science, and technology. It will also be remembered for death and destruction on a scale never seen before in human history. Millions died in World Wars I and II and in other wars. Millions more died at the hands of their own governments as totalitarian regimes brutally suppressed their people.

As a nation we have forgotten the true horror of war. Armies have not fought across our land since the American Civil War. We talk about the War on Cancer, the War on Drugs, and the War on Terrorism as if they are true wars. They are not. During World War II, some 50 million people died as a direct result of the war. That is as if everyone died in the states of Massachusetts, New Jersey, Virginia, Tennessee, Alabama, Oklahoma, Arizona, Oregon, Colorado, and Indiana. (Based on the 2000 Census.)

World War II is called by some the last good war. They are wrong. No war is good. Some wars, however, are necessary. The war that tore apart Europe and Asia during the 1930s and 1940s was a battle against three totalitarian states: Germany, Italy, and Japan. All three waged brutal wars of aggression. Although they differed from each other in the details of their internal organization and leadership, in the end all were based on the military power of the state. All three were also Fascist states.

Fascism should not be used as a general term for systems of government we do not like. It is a totalitarian form of government of the extreme political right. (The political right is the most conservative, reactionary element of a political system.) One of the keys to a Fascist state is the merging of business and government leadership. Government does not own the means of production, as it does under a Communist system. However, the leaders of business and government work together to control the nation and carry out their common goals. Fascism also generally involves an aggressive and belligerent form of nationalism. All three of the World War II Fascist states attacked other nations without provocation.

Fascist states also generally have a supreme leader supported by a political party and by a secret police organization that ensures the leader's control. They also build what we now call a cult of personality around the leader. In Japan, the leader was the God-Emperor Hirohito. In Germany, Adolf Hitler took the title of führer, which means "leader." In Italy, Benito Mussolini was also titled the leader, or Il Duce. In all three nations, uniformed thugs attacked and often killed opponents in the Fascists' drive for power. In Japan, the thugs were usually members of the army. In Germany, they were the Brown Shirts, the Nazi storm troopers of the Sturmabteilung (SA), or Assault Division. In Italy, the thugs wore black and were called the Black Shirts. Hitler and the Nazis put their own barbaric slant on Fascism with their racist and anti-Semitic ideology that lead to the Holocaust. The Holocaust saw the

murder of millions of people before the guns of death squads
and in camps that operated as factories of death.

Most of the time, we can say when a war starts. The
American Civil War began when Southern forces fired on Fort
Sumter in 1861. World War I began following the assassination of Austrian archduke Franz Ferdinand in 1914. But we do
not have an easy starting date for World War II. The war
started at different times for different nations.

The start of the war in Asia can be dated as far back as
1931 and Japan's invasion of Manchuria. (Although Manchuria
is now part of China, before World War II it was considered an
independent territory.) Most of the time, however, it is said to
have started in 1937 when Japan attacked China. In Europe,
the war began in 1939 when German troops crossed the
Polish border. Italy fought colonial wars in Ethiopia and
North Africa but did not really enter the World War until it
followed Germany in 1939. The United States came late to
the war. America's war began on December 7, 1941, when
Japan attacked the U.S. naval base at Pearl Harbor, Hawaii.
Following Japan's attack, Hitler ensured his destruction by
declaring war on America.

War was said by the German military writer
Clausewitz to be "the continuation of politics by and admix-
ture of other means." Clauswitz's phrase was morphed by
various writers into a statement that war was the continuation of diplomacy by military means. The modern view, however,
is that war marks the failure of politics and diplomacy. World
War II is often cited as a war that could have been prevented
by strong, early international action. Following World War I,

the nations of the world set up the League of Nations to prevent another Great War.

The League, however, was weak in structure and power. It was further weakened when the United States refused to join. Japan's attack on Manchuria and later on China was brought before the League of Nations. The League took no effective action to stop Japan. The League again failed to act effectively when Italy invaded Ethiopia in 1935, and when Germany reoccupied the Rhineland (a western part of Germany that borders France) early the next year. The final collapse of any effort to prevent war came when Great Britain and France allowed Hitler to seize part of Czechoslovakia at the Munich Conference late in 1938. The statement by British prime minister Neville Chamberlain following the Munich Conference that he had gained "peace in our time" has been ridiculed almost from the moment he spoke.

The passive acceptance of Japanese, Italian, and German aggression by the nations of the world in the years before the start of the war has been called appeasement. In other words, Britain, France, and other nations tried to prevent a world war by giving the aggressors what they wanted. The question that arises is whether or not Hitler or Japan could have been stopped in the late 1930s without a general war. Evidence from German generals after the war indicates that had Britain and France taken a strong stand when Hitler reoccupied the Rhineland or at the time of the Munich Conference, the army would have deposed him. Had Hitler fallen, Mussolini would most likely have contented himself with his colonial wars. The situation is less clear with Japan.

It is likely that Japan's military government would have had to fall to stop further Japanese aggression. The Japanese militarists might, however, have contented themselves with their war in China had Hitler not started the war in Europe.

The greatest failure of both Germany and Japan during the war had nothing to do with their military strategies. Both nations failed completely to place their industries on a war footing until the war was well underway. Britain alone was able to outproduce Germany. Once the industrial power of the United States and Russia joined the war, Germany, Italy, and Japan had lost. It took a great deal of death and destruction to make the Germans and Japanese realize they had lost, but neither had the industrial power to win a fight with America. The great tragedy is that 50 million people died before the Fascist states accepted their defeat.

World War II brings together four of the twentieth century's major trends. Above all, the war shows us the blood that drenched the past 100 years. World War II was the deadliest humanity has seen. The war also marks both the greatest success and final destruction of three of the century's totalitarian states. The war also helped bring about the fall of a fourth totalitarian state, the Soviet Union. Fascist and Communist states refined the methods of governmental control over the people of a nation. Fascist rule came and was defeated in Japan, Italy, and Germany. The loss of 20 million Russians in the war and the enormous economic cost of the war on the nation helped bring on the final collapse of the Soviet Union nearly fifty years later.

At the start of World War II, European colonial nations controlled most of the world. The economic, political, and human price of fighting World War II undercut Europe's ability to control its colonies. Within twenty years of the war's end, most colonies had become independent. Finally, the atomic bomb was created in the United States because of fear that Germany would soon build its own bomb. The bomb was used—for the first and, so far, the only time—on Japan in 1945. The United States, the Soviet Union, and other nations soon developed the hydrogen bomb and built arsenals holding thousands of bombs many times more powerful than those dropped on Japan.

World War II slips farther into our past, but the effects of the war are still with us. Think of only one possible change. If the atomic bomb had not been developed and used, there is a very good chance that the Allies would have had to invade Japan. Hundreds of thousands of American soldiers (and millions of Japanese) would have died. If your great grandfather was in the army or marines, there is a chance that he would have been killed. And if your great grandfather had died, you would likely not be here today. The past controls our present, just as our actions today determine your future and the future of your children.

Most of the selections in this anthology are primary sources. Primary sources are speeches, diaries, contemporary reports, and the like that show us the events from the point of view of the people who lived through those events. I have tried to give readers a broad understanding of World War II, from the earliest events that led to the war (Mussolini's establishment of the first Fascist state) through the end of the war and the dropping of the atomic bomb on

Japan. The chapter titles will be familiar, as they match many of the themes you have read about and discussed as part of your study of social studies.

CHAPTER ONE

Time, Continuity, and Change: Storm Clouds of War

"The March on Rome"
By Denis Mack Smith
From Mussolini
1982

During World War I, Italy fought with Great Britain, France, and the other Allies against Germany and Austria. The war was bloody for all nations involved, but it was especially hard on Italy. The nation lost 600,000 men, and many more were wounded. Italy had expected to earn control of some of Germany's overseas colonies by fighting with the Allies but performed so poorly in the war that it gained little. The war ended with Italy's economy devastated and with hundreds of thousands of unemployed former soldiers demanding change. Communism and Socialism spread rapidly among the disenchanted people seeking jobs. Unions grew. In reaction, conservative and business interests increasingly backed the new Fascist movement lead by Benito Mussolini, Il Duce.

Fascist Black Shirts fought a near civil war against Communists and Socialists. They also attacked moderate *union members and other opponents, helping spread the chaos and undermining a series of weak governments. Soon, bands of Black Shirts rampaged through large areas of Italy. Some Fascists wanted to seize power violently. Mussolini waited for the leaders of Italy to hand him power. After gaining power, Mussolini quickly turned Italy into a one-party totalitarian state. Italian Fascists took their name from the symbol of power used in ancient Rome, the bundle of rods surrounding an axe that was called the fasces. Mussolini proclaimed a new Roman Empire that would revive the glory of Italy. Instead, he led his nation to disaster.*

The selection below from historian Denis Mack Smith describes Mussolini's final rise to power and the failure of the democratic structure to stop him. The events Smith reports occurred in the fall of 1922.

Mussolini knew he had no hope if the army was ever ordered into action against the gathering rebellion and he therefore took pains to canvass support among officers and ex-officers. As well as three or four retired generals who were consulted about insurrectionary tactics, it is certain that many other senior, and still more junior, officers were sympathetic to his movement; yet it is unthinkable that the vast majority would ever have supported an armed rebellion against the king. The powerful "union of ex-combatants" was loyal and actively opposed to fascism. A former chief of staff of the army, General Badoglio, thought that fascism would crumble at the first shot after a bare dozen arrests, as did other ranking officers in a position to know.

After returning to Milan from Naples, Mussolini tried not to give the appearance that anything unusual was afoot. While some of his colleagues were quietly mobilising the squads for the final move, he rarely went to his office; he used to take drives in the country by day and go to the theatre by night, letting very few people know what he intended. In private, however, he talked to leading opinion-makers in Milan and convinced some at least that the economy would gain from having fascists in the government: he repeated that he wanted a balanced budget, a smaller bureaucracy, a more stable currency and reduced inflation. He naturally gave no hint of anything unpleasant in store for anyone. On the contrary he undertook that his blackshirt army would be disbanded after victory.

Meanwhile, other fascists kept in touch with the individual liberal leaders, giving each to understand severally and secretly that the fascists would be content with a modest representation in a coalition led by any one of them. Nor did former prime ministers think it improper to conduct such talks, though they knew Mussolini was building up a large private militia and using it for illegal purposes. [Luigi] Facta still refused to declare an emergency or recall army reservists, and on the evening of 27 October, when civil strife was obviously threatening, he rejected a request by the army commander in Rome, General Pugliese, to impose martial law. As the hours went by, Mussolini became ever more confident that the governing classes were reconciled to accepting almost anything he asked for.

During the night of 27–28 October, fascist squads began to occupy telephone exchanges and government offices, and just after midnight Facta at last agreed to act. The ministers, hastily summoned, agreed with him unanimously to advise the king to use the army, and Pugliese again assured them that the threatened insurrection would be crushed in a few hours. It cannot have crossed the ministers' minds that the king would depart from constitutional practice and reject their advice.

Vittorio Emanuele was a timid, enigmatic person who had no desire to play the unconstitutional king but had to admit that the liberal leaders had no answer to anarchy and parliamentary stalemate. Temperamentally he was drawn to anyone who would take firm decisions and control domestic unrest, especially if they also favoured imperial expansion and would stand up for Italian interests better than Orlando had done in negotiating the treaty of Versailles. Along with growing numbers of other responsible statesmen, he had come to accept that Mussolini's entry into the cabinet in a subordinate role might be the best way to resolve the political impasse. He saw his own chief duty as that of avoiding the outbreak of an armed revolution and he now threatened to abdicate in the event of civil war.

Early on 28 October, at about 2.00 a.m., the king was informed that insurrections had begun at Milan and elsewhere; he at once agreed with the cabinet's formal advice to declare a state of emergency and use the army to impose martial law. The necessary decree was hurriedly prepared. At breakfast time, the prime minister returned to secure the formality of the royal signature while the military went into action to crush the revolt. The fascists offered little resistance; buildings captured overnight were re-occupied and roads and railways blocked so that no march on Rome could take place. Not only the right-wing nationalist party, but even some of the fascist hierarchy including Cesare De Vecchi, one of the four designated commanders of the "march," declared that, faced by the choice, they would obey the king—there was talk of killing Mussolini if necessary.

Meanwhile in Milan at about 6.00 a.m., the fascist leader arrived at his office, barricaded by his staff as if for a siege. The army was already assuming full powers in the town without waiting for the official decree to be promulgated, and an order was drawn up for his arrest? However, in private discussions the fascists gave the prefect of Milan, Alfredo Lusignoli, to understand that he would be rewarded with a place in the cabinet if the order were ignored. Lusignoli's refusal to act was a crucial factor in the success of the rebellion. His motive was presumably ambition, or at least fear of losing his job if the fascists won, and no doubt some rich Milanese encouraged him.

Even more important was the king's change of mind—at some time before 9.00 a.m. he refused to sign the decree that he had accepted and indeed demanded a few hours previously. To refuse the recommendation of a cabinet, particularly a unanimous one, was an arbitrary breach of constitutional convention. But Vittorio Emanuele had no confidence in Facta's ability to control events; furthermore, he was privately advised not to sign by [Antonio] Salandra's friends who hoped that this would force Facta's resignation and give them the chance of forming a government. The king was also informed—privately, inaccurately, almost certainly with intent to deceive—that the army was outnumbered by fascist militiamen and could not defend Rome from attack.

His decision converted the fascists from outlaws into indispensable members of the next government. When Facta resigned, Salandra was invited to become prime minister and he asked Mussolini to join the new administration; but the latter refused, on the assumption that he could now name his own price. Salandra thereupon withdrew and, fearing that the choice might otherwise be [Giovanni] Giolitti, advised the king to appoint Mussolini—a man who was leading an armed rebellion against the state and whose private army was responsible for countless atrocities throughout Italy. On 29 October, the king accepted this advice and Mussolini, at the age of only thirty-nine, became the twenty-seventh prime minister of Italy.

But the fascist leader was not satisfied with something so unspectacular as a royal appointment. He needed to develop the myth of a march on Rome by 300,000 armed fascists to enforce an "ultimatum" he had given to the king, and eventually a legend was invented of Mussolini on horseback leading his legions across the Rubicon. In reality there were fewer than 30,000 fascist militiamen ready to march, many of whom had no arms at all and would have been quite unable to stand up to the garrison troops in Rome with their machine guns and armoured cars: indeed 400 policemen proved sufficient to hold up the fascist trains long before they reached Rome. Mussolini subsequently admitted this in private with amused satisfaction. His fascist squads did not arrive in Rome until twenty-four hours after he had been asked to form a government and only after General Pugliese had orders to let them through. But the photographers were waiting to picture their arrival and the myth was launched of fascism winning power by an armed insurrection after a civil war and the loss of 3,000 men. These fictitious 3,000 "fascist martyrs" soon took their place in the government-sponsored history books.

Mussolini did not hurry to leave Milan. He needed a few hours to organise a tumultuous send-off at the station and to give his counterfeit "march" time to get under way. To create an atmosphere of emergency, he announced that he was ready to govern by force—by machine gun if need be—and to show that he meant business he ordered his *squadristi* once again to destroy the printing machinery of opposition newspapers: it was important to prevent the general public from knowing anything except the fascist version of events. For a while he thought of leaving his sleeping car at a stop before Rome so that he could enter the city on horseback with a guard of blackshirts, but there was a risk of looking ridiculous, so he went the whole way by train and arrived during the morning of 30 October. His list of ministers, only a minority of whom were fascists, was accepted by the king that same evening. Rarely had a premier shown such speed and decision or found colleagues so immediately ready to join his cabinet.

By this time, the blackshirts had begun to arrive in Rome and some of the familiar violent episodes were taking place. The editor of at least one liberal paper was forced to drink the "fascist medicine," castor oil; socialist newspapers and bookstores were ransacked and heaps of books burnt in the street; shops were pillaged, houses belonging to political opponents broken into and foreign embassies compelled to fly the Italian flag. A number of private grievances were settled in the turmoil and a dozen people killed. Some fascists were disappointed that the casualties were not higher, and Mussolini subsequently made the comment that, in those "radiant days of October," he should have had more people put against a wall and shot.

Italy had become too numbed by a succession of outrages to be alarmed by this excess of high spirits. Though the lira fell drastically on the foreign bourses, the Italian stock market registered satisfaction at Mussolini's appointment. Marconi wired his congratulations; Giolitti and Salandra, the two senior members of the liberal establishment, expressed approval. Not even the extreme left was willing to react strongly. Mussolini had feared that a general strike might be proclaimed, which would create serious difficulties for him, but the socialist leaders remained passive; for years they had been looking forward to the collapse of the liberal state as a necessary step towards their own triumph. Whereas in Germany a strike checked the Kapp Putsch, in Italy the railwaymen made no difficulty about driving Mussolini's train to victory.

The absence of resistance implies that the public lacked confidence in the liberal leaders and was ready to accept the new government with resignation, if not pleasure. Fear of communism can have been only a minor motive as there was no communist threat. A much more realistic fear was felt by those among the wealthy who were concerned lest Giolitti return to power with a policy of high taxes and social reform.

Still more widespread was the feeling that fascism was an alternative to anarchy—the last resort, as it were, after parliament had failed to function in defence of law and order; few were troubled by the fact that the anarchy had been deliberately fanned by fascism itself. There were popular demonstrations of joy as Rome was swept by a holiday mood. Happy crowds paraded through streets decked with flags and demonstrated in front of the royal palace, applauding the king's decision not to invoke martial law. Foreign journalists reported that florists ran out of flowers as the city was overtaken by "a fever of delight" at the prospect of years of misgovernment coming to an end. These pro-fascist demonstrations, unlike most later ones, must have been spontaneous.

Last Train from Berlin
By Howard K. Smith
1942

Hitler built the National Socialist German Workers Party, the Nazis, with a mix of hate, fear, crackpot racial theories, and promises of renewed German glory. Hitler's street thugs, the SA, fought pitched battles in the streets of Germany against Hitler's political opponents—and against those people Hitler disliked. When the traditional German politicians and the industrial leaders of the nation agreed to make Hitler chancellor of Germany in January 1933, they thought he could be controlled. They were wrong. With control of the police, Hitler's thugs swept him to greater power. In March 1933, the Nazis and their allies in parliament passed the Enabling

Bill, which gave the government dictatorial powers. Hitler re-armed Germany and built a cult of German militarism and nationalism. It would take a long, bloody war to force the Nazis from power.

Howard K. Smith worked as a reporter for the United Press in Germany in the years before the war. He was the last reporter to leave the country before Germany and the United States declared war on each other in December 1941. He later worked for CBS Radio, reporting from England during the war. After the war, Smith reported for CBS and then ABC television. Smith was a Rhodes scholar studying at Oxford University in England when he first visited Germany in 1936. In his 1942 book, Last Train from Berlin, *Smith described the Germany he saw at the critical point midway between Hitler's rise to power and Germany's invasion of Poland.*

————□————

The first and most general of these passive impressions was good beyond all expectation. On first glance, Germany was overwhelmingly attractive, and first impressions disarmed many a hardy anti-Nazi before he could lift his lance for attack. Germany was clean, it was neat, a truly handsome land. Its big cities were cleaner than big cities ought, by custom, to be. You could search far and wide through Berlin's sea of houses or Hamburg's huge harbour district, but you could never find a slum or anything approaching one. On the countryside, broad, flourishing acres were cut into neat checkerboards, and no square foot of land was wasted. People looked good. Nobody was in rags, not a single citizen. They were well

dressed, if not stylishly dressed. And they were well fed. The
impression was one of order, cleanliness and prosperity—and
this has been of immense propaganda value to the Nazis.
There is a great fallacy here, and it is a mistake which an
unfortunately large number of young American students I
met in Heidelberg made and retained for a long time. The fallacy is in connecting this admirable order, cleanliness and
apparent prosperity with the Nazi government. Actually, and
this was pointed out to me by a German dock-worker on my
first magic day in Bremen, Germans and Germany were neat,
clean and able to do an amazing lot with amazingly little long
before Hitler came to power. Such slums as existed were
removed by the Socialist government and replaced with neat
workers' apartments while the Nazis were still a noisy minority
chalking swastikas on back-alley fences. The German people
are, by their very nature, clean and thrifty and can make their
Sunday suits last and look new for triple or quadruple the
time an American or an Englishman can. But no matter; that
is general impression number one to every visitor to Germany,
valid or not.

The second impression, a more specific one, followed
hard on the heels of the first, if it was not coeval with it. It
was—uniforms and guns; the amazing extent to which
Germany, even then, was prepared for war. It took my breath
away. I had read about Nazi rearmament, but to me it was still
a word, not a sense-idea. In New Orleans I could sum up in a
figure of two integers all the uniforms I had ever seen. Before
our boat docked in Bremen I saw a big multiple of that figure,
sailors of Germany's war navy, walking up and down the long

wharves. The railway station in Bremen, and later every railway station I saw, was a milling hive of soldiers in green uniforms in full war-kit and with rifles, getting off trains and getting on them. Farther inland, towns looked like garrisons, with every third or fourth man in uniform. On trains, all day long, one passed long railway caravans of camouflaged tanks, cannon and war-trucks lashed to railway flat cars, and freight depots were lined with more of these monsters hooded in brown canvas. In large towns, traffic had to be interrupted at intervals on some days to let cavalcades of unearthly machines, manned by dust-covered, steel-helmeted Men-from-Mars roar through the main streets in maneuvers.

The reaction that belongs to stage number two was one of titillation. Or, more than that, it was downright exciting. It was a brand new experience, rich in colour and thrilling action, to hoard up in my memory and describe later to wide-eyed, envious listeners at home.

Imagine the best example of it, standing at a window in Nuremberg, as I did later, watching a broad undulating river of ten, twenty thousand men in uniform, stamping in unison down the cobble-stone street below, flooding the valley between the houses with a marching song so loud the windows rattled, and so compelling your very heart adopted its military rhythm. In the thin margin between the houses and the men, helmeted messengers on motor-cycles sped up and down from mysterious grey staff cars ahead to staff cars in the rear, their cut-outs ripping raucous, jagged edges in the air. As far back as you could see were men in uniform, their ranks broken only occasionally by grey, motorized anti-aircraft guns nosing up at the sky; and you knew that beyond where you could see were thousands and thousands more.

Seeing vast numbers, great masses or infinite expanses, like a sea or an endless plain has a way of inducing philosophic moods and making one wonder about things like Time and Space and individual components of them. Seeing a mass of armed, uniformed men called into movement by a single laconic command, one inevitably began to grow curious about the individuals that made it up. Along these lines, in Germany, you could arrive at a new genus; *homo militaris*, it might be called. And you could with almost no active application, in that land where the genus abounds, observe and classify its "habits and customs" as a botanist observes and classifies flora. The outstanding property of the *homo militaris*, you discovered, is the readiness with which he can change personalities. For example, follow a couple of soldiers off duty down the street, any street in Germany. You admire their bronzed, smiling faces and the way they walk loosely and gracefully as athletes. They're completely human beings. Suddenly a certain stimulus is applied to the objects of study. For purposes of investigation, it might be called the stimulus of "officer in sight." In an instant, the two soldiers freeze into solid blocks of machinery; lightning-like they snap their arms, in unison, to their caps and their faces harden and lose expression. The stimulus is removed, the officer passes, and the young men collapse into humanity in an instant, and are again walking loosely and gracefully as athletes, as though nothing had happened.

Or take another example. In Heidelberg, on the parade ground outside the barracks. You stand and watch fifty or sixty of them drilling. Since you have lived there several weeks, and seen many of them on the streets, you know they are human beings. But on parade ground they have switched off humanity and are being trained for several hours at being machines. They react to incomprehensible, monosyllabic commands as a new slot-machine reacts to a shiny coin. They are simply having their reflexes drilled, so that they can move without thinking. On stimulus one they snap to rigid attention. On stimulus two they present arms. On stimulus three, all, like a single machine, raise their left legs high before them and begin goose-stepping. And you know that if stimulus four did not come to stop them, reaction three would carry them over a cliff, if one were there, and on the way down into the abyss, their expressionless faces would not change and their legs would click up and down in the air like a mechanical toy until they crashed at the bottom.

These were not observations for a dilettante. For they had meaning. As the novelty of anything inevitably wears off, so the novelty of militarism does with time. And as newness loses its grip on your faculties, your brain silently muscles in on territory that had belonged entirely to your senses. The impression is still a passive one; the thought process involved is no more active than a reverie. And this, in one form or another, is just the way almost every visitor to Germany I met slid imperceptibly from stage two of his passive impressions to stage three. You began to grasp that what was happening was that young humans, millions of them, were being trained to act merely upon reflexes. And you inevitably came to wonder, what, after all, is the ultimate, the final reflex toward which all this drilling is directed? Obviously, to kill, as a reflex. To destroy "according to plan." On terse commands which altered their personalities more neatly than Doctor Jekyll became Mr. Hyde, they were learning to smash, crush, destroy, wreck. Not one of them would harm a fly while he was Doctor Jekyll. But apply the proper stimulus and they would fall into the military trance, blast the guts out of the first person in range of them or drop big fat bombs on peaceful homes and blow them to smithereens. That, of course, is the nature of the military man in any country, but to understand their full effect, it must be remembered that these impressions came when the rest of the world, my nation in the fore, was sleeping in the delusion that its only problems were far less formidable than those of war. In that setting, the reaction that accompanies this stage is one of uneasiness . . .

A few months before, the Germans had, in defiance of the Versailles treaty, marched into the Rhineland. A friend of mine and I bicycled to Worms to see what we could see. The town was not in war, yet, but it was the best imitation of a town-in-war I have ever seen. The streets were filled with soldiers. On every corner forests of new sign-posts told the way to parking grounds for motorized units, regimental headquarters, divisional headquarters, corps headquarters, field hospitals. We elbowed our way the length of the main street and saw not another man in civilian dress. That evening we spent in a beer-hall, in whose upper stories we had rented rooms. The beer-hall was packed with fine-looking young officers, drinking, shouting, and singing. The tables were wet with spilled beer and the air hazy with blue cigarette smoke. I do not know what it was, except that the turn of this reaction was logically due—it was perhaps partly that the beer had loosened up my imagination—but watching the faces of these men, my own age, my own generation, caused me to think of their military culture, for the first time, in terms of me and my culture. For the first time I thought of Germany, not as an academic subject studiously to gather facts about for discussion at home, but as a real, direct and imminent threat to the existence of a civilization which gathers facts and discusses. A schism deeper than the Grand Canyon separated my world from that of the young man across from me, whose face bore fencing scars and carried a monocle over one glassy eye. The fetishes of my world, the values it worshipped, if it did not always attain them, were contained in words like "Reason," "Think," "Truth." His fetishes and his values were "Feel," "Obey," "Fight." There was no base pride for me in this involuntary comparison; rather, a terror like that which paralyzes a child alone in the dark took hold of me. For my world, with all the good qualities I thought it had, was, in terms of force, weak; his was mighty, powerful, reckless. It screamed defiance at my world from the housetops. One had to be deaf not to hear it.

After that my senses sharpened and I guided them to fill out my impressions. I watched propaganda in the newspapers, placards on street-corner billboards, listened to it on the radio; I took closer note of the trends and tone of lectures in Heidelberg, listened more attentively to conversations with university instructors, chosen for their ability as propagandists rather than as teachers, at Saturday night social gatherings in the Institute for Foreigners. Everything I saw and heard confirmed my new-born fear. I had now gone through all the stages save one—that is when fear has matured and been converted into political action. In its own way, that came later. The individual human will is a wonderful thing. It can accomplish deeds that are theoretically impossible, overcome serious illnesses, win governments. A nation of millions of human wills united in the determination to achieve a certain, definite end is that many times more powerful. A whole nation, for instance, which is unified as to means, methods, and an intense desire to abolish poverty and create abundance for all, could make the grandest civilization we have ever known, in a single generation. By the same token, a whole great nation which is unified in means, methods and will to carry out the single purpose of waging war could, if its neighbours were not equally determined, flood the world with blood and misery unequalled. That last is what I saw in Germany. I saw it before a month was out. My non-partisanship had slipped badly . . .

Government by Assassination
By Hugh Byas
1942

For nearly 700 years, Japan had been ruled by a series of military commanders, the shoguns. The emperor was only a figurehead. In 1858, the U.S. Navy's Commodore Matthew Perry forced Japan to open itself to the modern world. Ten years later, political parties rallied around Emperor Meiji and overthrew the shogun and local lords in the Meiji

Restoration. While Shinto was widely followed as a religion in Japan, the living emperor was not considered a god. The new rulers of Japan decided to build Shinto and the cult of the emperor into a religious foundation of the new Japan. In effect, they deified the emperor.

In 1931, the Japanese army—acting without approval from the government—marched into Manchuria and set up a puppet ruler. Throughout the 1930s, aggressive nationalists in the army systematically murdered moderate civilian and military leaders. The nationalists eventually took control of the nation and set up a Fascist regime.

Hugh Byas was an Englishman who lived in Japan throughout the 1930s. He wrote for the New York Times *and* The Times *(of London). His 1942 book,* Government by Assassination, *reports on the rise of the military to power in Japan. In the following selections, he discusses the cult of the emperor.*

———□———

THE EMPEROR OF JAPAN: AS GOD

When the Emperor Meiji, the first restored Emperor, lay dying in 1912, thousands of the citizens of Tokyo gathered nightly in front of the Palace and prayed for his recovery. Their prayers were directed to no other god than the divine ruler himself. I should not offer this statement on my own authority; mob emotion seems to me a better explanation than conscious belief in the godhood of a dying old man whose existence had been in no way remarkable, but it is the explanation given by Dr. Genji Kato, Professor of Comparative Religion at Tokyo Imperial University.

Imperial Shinto, or state-worship, the state being personified in the Emperor, was revived less than one lifetime ago by the leaders of the restoration-revolution, who needed some super-political sanction to foster political unity on the ruins of clan feudalism. Another eminent scholar, the late Basil Hall Chamberlain, wrote a pamphlet called The Invention of a New Religion describing the measures by which Imperial Shinto was set up side by side with the modern institutions the new Empire was then installing. Chamberlain, in effect, represented the leaders of new Japan as getting round a table and saying: "Let us invent a new religion, call it the ancient cult of Japan, and foist it upon the people so that we may more easily control them." But Chamberlain was of [Edward] Gibbon's opinion that all religions were considered by the people as equally true, by the philosopher as equally false, and by the government as equally useful. It is hard to reconcile his too rational explanation with the spectacle of those thousands of people praying in the snow. Even in Japan the government could not create a new religion in this self-conscious and fraudulent manner, and the idea of state-worship, of Japan as a unique and superior state with rulers of divine descent, had existed for many centuries. All that the government did was to turn this idea to its use, and it has grown to proportions which the Japanese statesmen of fifty years ago would not have believed had they been told.

Professor Kato claims for Shinto all the qualities of a major religion. The essence of any religion, he says, is "absolute trust in and complete self-surrender to the object of worship." The Japanese people, he continues, find this in Shinto because for them the Emperor is "God revealed in human form . . . occupying for the Japanese the place of the one whom the Jews called God." Dr. Kato places Shinto on the same plane as Buddhism and Christianity as a world religion. "If it is the boast of India that she produced the Buddha, and the boast of Judea that she counts among her sons Jesus the redeemer of the world, it is enough for Japan to boast that she has been from generation to generation under the sway of emperors who, in an unbroken line, ascended the throne of Imperial—that is to say, of divine—dignity."

He claims also that Shinto brings the world a supreme hope. The Jews, he says, cherished the hope of a political Messiah. When this hope failed it was transferred to the spiritual sphere and Christianity extended its moral dominion over many nations. If Buddha had been willing to accept political supremacy this might have been India's mission, but he too turned aside to spiritual leadership. Dr. Kato continues: "The great Messianic ideal which those ancient nations vainly longed for the Japanese possess, and thus we see, rising in the Eastern heavens, that great hope of humanity, Messiah the Ruler."

Dr. Kato is no patriotic or military windbag, nor is he a bigot. He is a scholar of high rank, and his work is well known to foreign scholars: His book *Waga Kokutai to Shinto (Our National Structure and Shinto)* closes with a touching appeal to Christians to come together with the Japanese "in the spirit of religious brotherhood in one assembly hall and, making no mention of Buddhism or Christianity or Shinto, clasp one another's hands." There is no greater authority on Japanese religion, and when Dr. Kato claims that Emperor-worship is a religion in the fullest sense of the word, and not merely a ceremonial manifestation of loyalty, as Japanese apologists have represented it, we must respect his opinion. Yet, as a layman, speaking only from long observation of Japanese life, I must record my own opinion that Dr. Kato's description is an overstatement.

It is not merely a question of the eternal difference between the devout and the indifferent. For every Japanese who prayed in the slush to the dying Emperor, ten thousand stayed at home. That proves nothing; we would have to say the same of many other religious communities. But there is a fundamental difference between the god the Japanese prays to and the God the Christian or the Jew prays to. Shinto began as nature-worship; it saw a god in every natural force and it worshipped the spirits of the woods, of the rice fields, of the tides, of fire, of water, of everything. Ancestor-worship was imported from China and incorporated. There is something to be said for the theory that the early rulers, claiming descent from the Sun Goddess, caused that deity to be set above the Food Goddess in order to strengthen their own position.

The conception of one God, who made and rules the universe and who alone is divine and worthy of worship, has no place in the Shinto scheme of things. To the Christian, the Jew, the Mohammedan, God is above and apart from the world that he made; to the Shintoist, as to all pantheists, godhood manifests itself in the world and is part of the world. The Emperor is the god of Japan; he is part of Japan; his father was a god before him, and his son will be a god after him. One need not be a theologian to see that when a Japanese says the Emperor is god, he means something different from the Christian.

But the Emperor is the only god he has. When children go to school on New Year's morning and see the portraits of the Emperor and Empress brought from their sanctuary with the reverence the Christian shows to the consecrated bread and wine, they are not worshipping an eternal father, their creator and redeemer; they are worshipping the Japanese Empire.

Dr. Kato is not a political philosopher or he would have seen that such a religion exalts and justifies unbounded aggression. Some newer forms of Shinto have taken the step which Dr. Kato did not see. Starting from the divinity of the Emperor, they claimed that Japan, by right of its unique and inherent qualities, should become the dominant power of the world, with the Imperial family as the new Messiah. An American missionary and scholar, the late Dr. Albertus Pieters quoted the following utterance of one of the new nationalist Shinto sects:

"Japan is the parent nation of the world. He who is hostile to this nation opposes the will of God." And again: "The Imperial family of Japan is the parent not only of the Japanese race but of all the nations on earth. In the eyes of the Imperial family all races are the same. It is above all racial considerations. All human disputes therefore may be settled in accordance with its immaculate justice. The League of Nations can only attain its object by placing the Imperial family of Japan at its head, for, if it is to succeed, the League must have a strong punitive force of a super-racial and super-national character and this can only be found in the Imperial family of Japan."

In some of its manifestations the "divinity" of the Japanese Emperor seems to be the sign of an inferiority complex so morbid that it cannot bear the thought of Japan being governed or reigned over by a human being as other countries are. Count Yoshinori Futara (who had a modern education, including foreign travel) discussed the question whether loyalty to the Emperor had diminished or increased during the reign of Taisho (1912–26), Hirohito's immediate predecessor. He thought its essence still survived despite the skepticism of a modern age. Japan of our day, he wrote, began to regard the Emperor as simply a person and young men thought the emperors of the past were historical personages. They therefore respected the present Emperor at the beginning of his reign as an august person who ascended the throne by right of birth. But this, continues Count Futara, "is quite inconsistent with the racial ideal of Japan. The Emperor who should reign over us eternally from time immemorial to the endless future must not be regarded as merely an august personage, he should be venerated as a superhuman existence."

The national megalomania, of which worship of the Emperor was a symptom, was not taken seriously by other nations. Japan was far away on the rim of Asia and the white world undervalued it. The amiable Japanese who were Japan's contact-men with the West described Emperor-worship as a simple cult of loyalty wearing the garments of a quaint and ancient civilization. They did not say, because they did not see, that Japan's religion was a new paganism whose inherent barbarism would in no long time plunge Asia into bloody wars.

[After describing the role of the emperor as high priest of the state religion, Shinto, and providing additional background,

Hugh Byas reported how the emperor became the symbol for the ultra-nationalists.]

The final results of Hitlerism to Germany will not greatly differ from the final results Japan will draw from the insensate nationalism of her Emperor-worship.

Yet this abject glorification of the Imperial figurehead is a modern invention. The title "Son of Heaven" only became official on June 1, 1936. It seems to have been first used officially of a living Emperor in the Constitution of 1890; before then it had been reserved for dead emperors. And before 1868 emperors living or dead had counted for little in government. The first treaties Japan ever made were made in the name of the Tycoon. The first document signed and issued in modern times by a Japanese monarch was an announcement by the Emperor Meiji on January 31, 1868, telling foreign diplomats that henceforth the title of Emperor was to be substituted for that of Tycoon in the treaties. One historian declares that that was the first occasion on which the name of an emperor had appeared during his lifetime.

The clan statesmen of the nineteenth century who made the Constitution deliberately surrounded the Imperial dynasty with the mystic emotional halos and sanctions that accompany divinity and divine origin. They did so to create unity in support of a regime they had established after a revolution. By identifying the ruling house with the gods they were using religious myth to prevent the growth of democratic ideas, then making headway. They achieved in the popular mind a complete fusion of political with religious and theocratical ideas. The fusion of religion and nationalism resulted in the hypertrophied

ambition which is trying to subjugate Asia. It has elevated
the power and prestige of the dynasty till human emperors
are worshipped as gods, by all the benefit of this power and
prestige has accrued to the fighting services and the bureau-
crats who actually exercise it. The Emperor is god, high
priest, symbol, figurehead; power is still "the prerogative of
the high command."

Berlin Diary: The Journal of a Foreign Correspondent, 1934–1941
By William L. Shirer
1941

*The German military occupation of the Rhineland in 1936
was one of several major opportunities the British and
French had to stop Hitler's drive for war. The Treaty of
Versailles, signed after World War I, had a number of provisions designed to limit Germany's military power and to
protect Germany's neighbors from attack. The Rhineland
demilitarized zone was the westernmost portion of Germany.
(Mainly, it is the valley of the Rhine River.) Allied troops
were to occupy the Rhineland for fifteen years. (The British
troops withdrew in 1926, followed by the French in 1930.)
While it was part of Germany, no German troops were ever
to enter the Rhineland. The 1925 Treaty of Locarno reaf-
firmed the demilitarization of the Rhineland and the borders
of Germany and its neighbors. The Treaty of Locarno was
signed by Germany, France, and Belgium, and by Britain
and Italy as "guarantors" of the treaty.*

*After renouncing the provisions of the Treaty of Versailles
that limited the size of the German military in March 1935,
Hitler waited a year before moving into the Rhineland.
Following the announcement of a defense agreement between
Russia and France and after the start of the Italian-Ethiopian
war, Hitler renounced the Treaty of Locarno. He sent about
10,000 troops—only three battalions—to reoccupy the
Rhineland. France had 250,000 troops mobilized and the
British and French air forces could easily have attacked the
German troops. But France and Britain did nothing.*

*William L. Shirer was in Berlin as a correspondent for
CBS Radio. He reports events in the selection from his* Berlin
Diary *printed below. In the diary, Shirer reported that the
German army was prepared to withdraw if the French or
British took any military action against them. His report was
confirmed after the war by testimony from German generals
at the Nuremberg war crimes trials.*

———□———

BERLIN, March 7

A little on the careful side is right! Hitler on this day has
torn up the Locarno Treaty and sent in the Reichswehr [the
German army] to occupy the demilitarized zone of the
Rhineland! A few diplomats on the pessimistic side think it
means war. Most think he will get by with it. The important
thing is that the French army has not budged. Tonight for
the first time since 1870 [the Franco-Prussian War] grey-
clad German soldiers and blue-clad French troops face each
other across the upper Rhine. But I talked to Karlsruhe [a
German city near the French border] on the phone an hour

ago; there have been no shots. I've had our Paris office on the line all evening, filing my dispatch. They say the French are not mobilizing—yet, at least—though the Cabinet is in session with the General Staff. London—as a year ago— seems to be holding back. The Reichswehr generals are still nervous, but not so nervous as they were this morning.

To describe this day, if I can:

At ten o'clock this morning Neurath handed the ambassadors of France, Britain, Belgium, and Italy a long memorandum. For once we got a break on the news because Dr. Dieckhoff, the State Secretary in the Foreign Office, called in Freddy Mayer, our counsellor of Embassy, and gave him a copy of the memorandum, apparently suggesting he give it to the American correspondents, since the American Embassy rarely gives us a lift like this of its own accord. Huss, who needed an early report for the INS, hurried over to the Embassy, and I walked over to the Reichstag, which was meeting at noon in the Kroll Opera House. The memorandum, however, along with Neurath's oral remarks to the army that German troops had marched into the Rhineland at dawn this morning, told the whole story.

It argued that the Locarno pact had been rendered "extinct" by the Franco-Soviet pact, that Germany therefore no longer regarded itself as bound by it, and that the "German Government has therefore, as from today, restored the full and unrestricted sovereignty of the Reich in the demilitarized zone of the Rhineland." There followed then another beautiful attempt by Hitler—and who can say he won't succeed, after May 21 last?—to throw sand in the

eyes of the "peace-loving" men of the West, men like
Londonderry, the Astors, Lord Lothian, Lord Rothermere.
He proposed a seven-point program of "Peace" in order, as
the memo puts it, "to prevent any doubt as to its [the Reich
government's] intentions, and to make clear the purely
defensive character of this measure, as well as to give
expression to its lasting desire for the true pacification of
Europe. . . ." The proposal is a pure fraud, and if I had any
guts, or American journalism had any, I would have said so in
my dispatch tonight. But I am not supposed to be "editorial."

In this latest "peace proposal" Hitler offers to sign a
twenty-five-year non-aggression pact with Belgium and
France, to be guaranteed by Britain and Italy; to propose to
Belgium and France that *both* sides of their frontiers with
Germany be demilitarized; to sign an air pact; to conclude
non-aggression pacts with her eastern neighbours; and,
finally, to return to the League of Nations. The quality of
Hitler's sincerity may be measured by his proposal to demili-
tarize *both* sides of the frontiers, thus forcing France to
scrap her Maginot Line, now her last protection against a
German attack.

The Reichstag [German parliament], more tense than I
have ever felt it (apparently the hand-picked deputies on the
main floor had not yet been told what had happened, though
they knew something was afoot), began promptly at noon. The
French, British, Belgian, and Polish ambassadors were
absent, but the Italian was there and [U.S. Ambassador
William E.] Dodd. General von Blomberg, the War Minister,
sitting with the Cabinet on the left side of the stage, was as

white as a sheet and fumbled the top of the bench nervously with his fingers. I have never seen him in such a state. Hitler began with a long harangue which he has often given before, but never tires of repeating, about the injustices of the Versailles Treaty and the peacefulness of Germans. Then his voice, which had been low and hoarse at the beginning, rose to a shrill, hysterical scream as he raged against Bolshevism.

"I will not have the gruesome Communist international dictatorship of hate descend upon the German people! This destructive Asiatic *Weltanschauung* [philosophy] strikes at all values! I tremble for Europe at the thought of what would happen should this destructive Asiatic conception of life, this chaos of the Bolshevist revolution, prove successful!"

Then, in a more reasoned voice, his argument that France's pact with Russia had invalidated the Locarno Treaty. A slight pause and:

"Germany no longer feels bound by the Locarno Treaty. In the interest of the primitive rights of its people to the security of their frontier and the safeguarding of their defence, the German Government has re-established, as from today, the absolute and unrestricted sovereignty of the Reich in the demilitarized zone!"

Now the six hundred deputies, personal appointees all of Hitler, little men with big bodies and bulging necks and cropped hair and pouched bellies and brown uniforms and heavy boots, little men of clay in his fine hands, leap to their feet like automatons, their right arms upstretched in the Nazi salute, and scream "*Heil's*," the first two or three wildly, the next twenty-five in unison, like a college yell. Hitler raises his hand for silence. It comes slowly. Slowly the automatons sit down. Hitler now has them in his claws. He appears to sense it. He says in a deep, resonant voice: "Men of the German Reichstag!" The silence is utter.

"In this historic hour, when in the Reich's western provinces German troops are at this minute marching into their future peace-time garrisons, we all unite in two sacred vows."

He can go no further. It is news to this hysterical "parliamentary" mob that German soldiers are already on the move into the Rhineland. All the militarism in their German blood surges to their heads. They spring, yelling and crying, to their feet. The audience in the galleries does the same, all except a few diplomats and about fifty of us correspondents. Their hands are raised in slavish salute, their faces now contorted with hysteria, their mouths wide open, shouting, shouting, their eyes, burning with fanaticism, glued on the new god, the Messiah. The Messiah plays his role superbly. His head lowered as if in all humbleness, he waits patiently for silence. Then, his voice still low, but choking with emotion, utters the two vows:

"First, we swear to yield to no force whatever in the restoration of the honour of our people, preferring to succumb with honour to the severest hardships rather than to capitulate. Secondly, we pledge that now, more than ever, we shall strive for an understanding between European peoples, especially for one with our western neighbour nations . . . We have no territorial demands to make in Europe! . . . Germany will never break the peace."

It was a long time before the cheering stopped. Down in the lobby the deputies were still under the magic spell, gushing

over one another. A few generals made their way out. Behind
their smiles, however, you could not help detecting a nervous-
ness. We waited in front of the Opera until Hitler and the
other bigwigs had driven away and the S.S. guards would let
us through. I walked through the Tiergarten with John Elliott
to the Adlon, where we lunched. We were too taken aback to
say much.

There is to be an "election" on March 29, "so the
German people may pass judgment on my leadership," as
Hitler puts it. The result, of course, is a foregone conclusion,
but it was announced tonight that Hitler will make a dozen
"campaign" speeches starting tomorrow.

[Editor's note: For about a page, Shirer discusses writing
his news dispatches. He also reports that the Germans
claimed to have used about 10,000 troops in the Rhineland.
He estimates they used 50,000 men. After the war, the
German number was confirmed as accurate.]

And so goes the main pillar of the European peace structure, Locarno. It was freely signed by Germany, it was not a
Dictat, and Hitler more than once solemnly swore to respect
it. At the Taverne tonight one of the French correspondents
cheered us up by stating positively that the French army
would march tomorrow but after what our Paris office said
tonight I doubt it. Why it doesn't march, I don't understand.
Certainly it is more than a match for the Reichswehr. And if it
does, that's the end of Hitler. He's staked all on the success of
his move and cannot survive if the French humiliate him by
occupying the west bank of the Rhine. Around the Taverne's
Stammtisch [a table reserved for regular guests] most of us

agreed on this. Much beer and two plates of spaghetti until three a.m., and then home. Must get up in time to attend another Heroes Memorial Day service at the Opera tomorrow. It should be even better than last year—unless the French—

BERLIN, March 8

Hitler has got away with it! France is not marching. Instead it is appealing to the League! No wonder the faces of Hitler and Goring and Blomberg and Fritsch were all smiles this noon as they sat in the royal box at the State Opera and for the second time in two years celebrated in a most military fashion Heroes Memorial Day, which is supposed to mark the memory of the two million Germans slain in the last war.

Oh, the stupidity (or is it paralysis?) of the French! I learned today on absolute authority that the German troops which marched into the demilitarized zone of the Rhineland yesterday had strict orders to beat a hasty retreat if the French army opposed them in any way. They were not pre-pared or equipped to fight a regular army. That probably explains Blomberg's white face yesterday. Apparently Fritsch (commander-in-chief of the Reichswehr) and most of the gen-erals opposed the move, but Blomberg, who has a blind faith in the Führer and his judgment, talked them into it. It may be that Fritsch, who loves neither Hitler nor the Nazi regime, consented to go along on the theory that if the coup failed, that would be the end of Hitler; if it succeeded, then one of his main military problems was solved.

Another weird story today. The French Embassy says— and I believe it—that [Francois] Poncet [the French ambassador to Berlin] called on Hitler a few days ago and asked him to propose his terms for a Franco-German rapprochement. The Führer asked for a few days to think it over. This seemed reasonable enough to the Ambassador, but he was puzzled at Hitler's insistence that no word leak out to the public of this visit. He is no longer puzzled. It would have spoiled Hitler's excuse that France was to blame for his tearing up the Locarno Treaty if the world had known that France, which after all had not yet ratified the Soviet pact, was willing to negotiate with him—indeed, had asked to negotiate.

CHAPTER TWO

PEOPLE, PLACES, AND ENVIRONMENTS: WORLD REACTION TO WORLD WAR

"Letters from the Manchurian Border" (part 1) and "The War that Is Not War" (part 2)
By Nora Waln
From The Atlantic Monthly
May and June 1932

World War II started in Europe in 1939 when Germany invaded Poland. But World War II had been raging in Asia since 1937 when Japan invaded China. By some analysis, the war started in 1931 when Japan seized Manchuria, the northernmost part of China. Japan had occupied Korea after the Russo-Japanese War in 1905. By 1931, Japan had a large army in Manchuria protecting Japanese interests.

While the Japanese government was controlled by militarists, they were waiting for an excuse to seize Manchuria. The extremists of Japan's Kwantung Army acted on their own. On September 19, 1931, they blew up part of the South Manchurian Railroad and blamed the army of the warlord who ruled Manchuria for China. With

that excuse, Japan took control of the capital, Mukden
(which is now called Shenyang) and then the rest of
Manchuria. The Japanese government eventually backed
the army, and any hope of civilian control of the military in
Japan died. Japanese troops attacked areas of northern
China and landed at Shanghai. The failure of the League of
Nations to stop Japan sped the coming of world war. In
February 1932, Japan turned Manchuria into a puppet
state of Manchukuo.

In 1937, Japanese aircraft bombed a U.S. Navy gun-
boat near the Chinese city of Nanking. In December of that
year, Japan captured the city. The resulting destruction was
called the Rape of Nanking. More than 300,000 Chinese
died, most butchered in the streets by Japanese troops.
Between 20,000 and 80,000 women were raped. Japan's
brutality was largely responsible for turning Americans from
friends to enemies.

The following selection is from a 1932 article, "Letters
from the Manchurian Border," sent to The Atlantic Monthly
by American writer Nora Waln. (In 1933, Waln published a
book reporting her life in China, The House of Exile.) Waln
had moved to China in 1920. She lived as a guest in a
Chinese household where she spoke only Chinese. She mar-
ried a British diplomat in China and continued to live in the
country for more than ten years. At the time of the Japanese
attack on Manchuria in 1931, Waln lived in the International
Zone of Tientsin (now Tianjin) southwest of Beijing. She
reports on both Japanese actions and the effort of people to
continue their lives as war closed in on them.

——□——

Tientsin, September 29, 1931

The Japanese occupation of Mukden, the seat of the
Manchurian government, was accomplished quickly and quietly,
and met with practically no opposition. The very quietness
with which the whole thing was accomplished, as well as the
swift flight of the familiar Chinese officials, alarmed the populace. But Japan, it seems, does not want the Chinese settlers
to leave. Japanese spokesmen attempted to calm the people by
assuring them that it would be best for them to remain in
their shops and on their farms. When this proved insufficient
to check the exodus, Japan decided to fight fear with fear,
making the Chinese settlers more afraid to return than to stay.
This strategy was carried out by having airplanes follow the
refugee trains and drop bombs on them.

I had heard Manchurian refugees tell about this at
Tientsin's East Station, and I had also read it in the papers;
still I was doubtful. Then Madame Accurti arrived to confirm
the story with direct testimony. She is the Frenchwoman
who owns and manages Fleurette, the only good dress shop
here. She goes to Paris by the Siberian route each spring
and autumn, and is entirely depended upon to purchase
complete outfits suitable to the needs and personalities of
her customers, and at prices proportionate to their means.
She returned by train No. 102 out of Mukden on the twenty-
sixth. She had with her two English children whom she had
agreed to fetch from London and escort to their parents in
Tientsin. At the Mukden Station she conversed with the
nephew of Tientsin's principal Indian silk merchant, who

told her that he had been closing up his uncle's Mukden branch.

She noticed a Japanese airplane flying overhead shortly after the train pulled out of Mukden, but thought nothing of it. Then about thirty miles out the plane began to drop bombs. Even then she supposed that they were blanks, and was so completely unaware of the danger that she let the children lean out to observe how skillfully the pilot maneuvered back and forth, right over the cars. Almost immediately the train was hit and came to a halt, while bombs continued to explode. A Chinese mother with a baby in her arms was struck and decapitated; her head rolled one way and the infant the other. The Indian merchant's nephew was killed. Madame Accurti covered the English children's eyes with bandages to keep them from seeing the horrors.

As quickly as it began, it was over. The bombing stopped. Madame Accurti leaned from the car window and saw the airplane flying back toward Mukden.

After a while the train went on, the unhurt passengers doing what they could for the injured. . . .

TIENTSIN, November 13, 1931

The rumble of field-gun fire and the rat-a-tat of rifle shot have been incessant all night . . .

Ever since the Japanese took over Mukden, the rumor has been voiced innumerable times a day that 'to-night Japan will march on Tientsin.' The American, British, French, Swedish, Belgian, German, and Italian Consuls have taken the rumor sufficiently seriously to meet together frequently and make plans for such an emergency. Several times they have jointly advised both the Japanese Consul General and the general in charge of the Japanese forces here that they think such action unwise, if 'contemplated.'

Among my acquaintances at Tientsin, all the Chinese people of every class, except the students, are united in favor of non-resistance against Japan. They trust in the League of Nations to investigate and effect a fair settlement . . .

Ever since Japan took possession of Mukden in September, I have been unable to go out for an hour without meeting Japanese with notebooks in their hands, earnestly jotting things down. They move about in groups of two or three. At the railway stations, by the bridges, on the Bund, in the food markets, in the streets, in the shops—everywhere they are to be seen industriously setting down their mysterious observations. They are quiet enough, but I do not like their being here.

One of them stared at me so hard while I sat talking to my friend, the coppersmith, that I contrived to see what he was putting into his book, and found that he had done a sketch of me with some Japanese writing under it. He was a little man, not as high as my shoulder, so when I came upon him making other notes farther up the street I reached out suddenly and took the book from his hand. He sputtered his surprise, but made no complaint when I tore out the page bearing the sketch of me. I handed the book back, and he bowed politely.

According to the vernacular press, up and down trains between here and Mukden are delayed several hours each way by Japanese officials at Hsinminfu and Hsinglungtao. Chinese men and women are ruthlessly disrobed to the waist and vulgarly searched for any letters or papers that may be concealed in their clothing or luggage. The reason given is that all communication has been forbidden between individuals at Mukden and Chang lisuch-liang at Peking or his brother, Chang Hsueh-ming, Mayor of Tientsin, [These brothers are sons of the late Chang Tso-lin, who was dictator of Manchuria. Chang Hsueh-liang, the older brother, inherited his father's rights to the dictatorship. . . .] but people, often disguised as women of good family, go in and out of Manchuria carrying messages.

Two Americans, Ben Dorfman of the University of California and Edward Hunter of Peking, have confirmed these reports. The railway authorities, seeing that these examinations were discouraging traffic and cutting down receipts, hoped to put a stop to them by making the matter public, and the two Americans to make an investigation. On October 21 they managed to take photographs of such an examination, but were immediately arrested, at the point of bayonets, by Japanese soldiers. They were held an hour before the American Consulate secured their release.

Part 2: The War that Is Not War
TIENTSIN, Saturday, November 14, 1931

This is the fifty-seventh night since Japan ungloved the mailed fist in Manchuria, and the sixth since the initial outburst of guns at Tientsin. Except for infrequent sniper fire and the occasional rumble of cannon to the northwest, the night has been quiet.

As I settled into my seat at the Tientsin Gayety Theatre at nine-thirty, I found the concert hall but sparsely peopled. I knew that the seats had all been sold. Yet, in view of the barbed wire, sandbags, earth dugouts, concealed trenches, machine guns, tanks, and steel-helmeted sentries with bayonet rifles, placed not only by China and Japan, but by all the Western nations permitted by treaty to have soldiers in China, across the thoroughfares and passageways to challenge, in the name of martial law, the right of civilians to move from one place to another—in view of all this, we who succeeded in getting to the concert were a goodly number. Americans, Britons, Frenchmen, Germans, Belgians, Russians, both White and Red, Italians, Danes, Swedes, Norwegians, Swiss, Chinese, Japanese—our cosmopolitan community was represented in the audience, with no nationality predominant. We were mostly feminine, also mostly middle-aged. Youth has faith to wait for easier conditions to attend concerts. We who have seen more of life take things as they come. Our men, for the most part, were elsewhere, their attentions entirely occupied with what was described, not as war, but as "a delicate situation." . . .

We were taut with waiting for the crisis, which is harder than meeting it directly; fatigued by caring for the wounded and by duty in refugee soup kitchens; too experienced in war to have any illusions about the power of battle to settle the dispute; too well read in treaties to have any faith in the power of the League of Nations; too versed in economics to believe that disinterested idealism could now enter the arena of world politics. In short, we were an audience of women whose national suspicion of one another was concealed behind courteous bows and smiles.

The auditorium lights went out; the stage lights went on. Jascha Heifetz walked forward. He lifted his violin and settled it with care. He raised his bow. The first number listed on the programme was the *Allegro molto ed appassionato* of Grieg's sonata for the piano and violin in C minor. My ears strained for the opening note, but it did not come. Heifetz had sensed the unnatural tension that gripped his audience. He lifted his head and stood for a moment like some startled, sensitive creature of the woods. He put down his instrument, stepped back, and half turned to Isidor Achnon at the piano. After a long pause he advanced resolutely to the footlights again and began to play— not the advertised programme but a divine idealism which he seemed to summon forth, not from the strings of his violin, but from our own taut nerves.

Hour after hour far into the night, without rest and without applause, he flung his spirit out to succor us. When the stage lights went off and the auditorium lights went on again, we were no longer scattered over the hail. We had crept in close together. We were women with wet eyes, clinging to each other's hands. We could not answer him, so we slipped away. My exit was blocked by two neighbors who stood in my aisle—one Chinese, one Japanese, both the wives of generals. They were staring into each other's faces. Tears ran unheeded over the careful make-up of each countenance.

I made my two miles home through passages empty except for the tools of war and other women who, like me, were scuttling home from the concert. I was challenged at frequent intervals by sentries . . . sentries with pointed bayonets—stationed twelve abreast across what was formerly Kaiser Wilhelm Street and is now called Woodrow Wilson Street . . . sentries of different nationalities, most of them courteous, many quite young, each somebody's husband or sweetheart or son. All looked so tired and cold that every time I met one I wished I had a magic pot of hot coffee so that I could give him a warming drink. Dawn was painting the sky as I pounded for admittance on the stout barred gates set in the high stone wall around my residence. . . .

TIENTSIN, November 20, 1931

Today I witnessed a "long winter coat" incident. Ever since the beginning of trouble here the Rotarians and the Chambers of Commerce have been trying to convince the military authorities that martial law not only was imposing terrible hardships on the populace but was also bankrupting big business, so on the seventeenth it was announced that martial law would be lifted for five hours daily. To-day I took advantage of the new edict to go shopping in the southwestern part of the Chinese city, at Hsi Kung Kai. The writing-paper shopkeeper was just bidding me the usual courteous farewell in his doorway when he suddenly whispered, "Look to the north!"

Twenty men in long new winter coats filed solemnly out of an alley into the crowded street. They held rifles at arm's length above their heads and shot them off into the sky. There was an immediate panic and the police started shooting. On the pavement near us two pedestrians—a woman and a child—fell with blood staining their clothes. They were carried into the shop, where I helped to dress their wounds. The news spread that we knew how to stop blood, and a policeman with a bullet in his leg was brought to us. The capable wife of the shopkeeper supplied cloth for bandages, kept the clerks boiling water, made beds on the counters for the wounded, and with cups of green tea quieted the frightened folk who crowded in for safety. . . .

Haile Selassie's Speech to the League of Nations
June 30, 1936
Geneva, Switzerland

Italy was late to the colonial feeding frenzy to dismember Africa. By 1914, Italy had only three colonies in Africa: Libya in North Africa, Eritrea on the Red Sea coast north of Ethiopia, and Italian Somaliland on the southern shore of the Horn of Africa. Italy had been trying for decades to take over Ethiopia. In 1896, the Ethiopians defeated an Italian army of 20,000 at Aduwa.

Benito Mussolini and the Italian Fascists had seized power in 1922. Mussolini said he would build a new Roman Empire and poured money into the Italian military. By 1934, Mussolini wanted military glory. In December, a clash on the border between Ethiopia and Italian Somaliland gave him an excuse. More than 300,000 Italian troops invaded Ethiopia in

October 1935, using armored vehicles, airplanes, and mustard gas. Tens of thousands of Ethiopian soldiers and civilians died. Ethiopia appealed to the League of Nations, which voted sanctions against Italy. The League did not, however, block oil shipments to Italy. The sanctions were not enforced and the League and the nations of Europe proved unable and unwilling to stop Italy's aggression. After being forced into exile, Emperor Haile Selassie of Ethiopia appeared at the League. He recounted the events of the war and warned the nations of Europe that war might come to them next.

———□———

[Editor's note: Haile Selassie's introductory paragraph has been omitted.] At the beginning, towards the end of 1935, Italian aircraft hurled upon my armies bombs of tear-gas. Their effects were but slight. The soldiers learned to scatter, waiting until the wind had rapidly dispersed the poisonous gases. The Italian aircraft then resorted to mustard gas. Barrels of liquid were hurled upon armed groups. But this means also was not effective; the liquid affected only a few soldiers, and barrels upon the ground were themselves a warning to troops and to the population of the danger.

It was at the time when the operations for the encircling of Makalle were taking place that the Italian command, fearing a rout, followed the procedure which it is now my duty to denounce to the world. Special sprayers were installed on board aircraft so that they could vaporize, over vast areas of territory, a fine, death-dealing rain. Groups of nine, fifteen, eighteen aircraft followed one another so that the fog issuing from them formed a continuous sheet. It was thus that, as from the end of January, 1936, soldiers, women, children, cattle, rivers, lakes and pastures were drenched continually with this deadly rain. In order to kill off systematically all living creatures, in order to more surely poison waters and pastures, the Italian command made its aircraft pass over and over again. That was its chief method of warfare.

Ravage and Terror

The very refinement of barbarism consisted in carrying ravage and terror into the most densely populated parts of the territory, the points farthest removed from the scene of hostilities. The object was to scatter fear and death over a great part of the Ethiopian territory. These fearful tactics succeeded. Men and animals succumbed. The deadly rain that fell from the aircraft made all those whom it touched fly shrieking with pain. All those who drank the poisoned water or ate the infected food also succumbed in dreadful suffering. In tens of thousands, the victims of the Italian mustard gas fell. It is in order to denounce to the civilized world the tortures inflicted upon the Ethiopian people that I resolved to come to Geneva. None other than myself and my brave companions in arms could bring the League of Nations the undeniable proof. The appeals of my delegates addressed to the League of Nations had remained without any answer; my delegates had not been witnesses. That is why I decided to come myself to bear witness against the crime perpetrated against my people and give Europe a warning of the doom that awaits it, if it should bow before the accomplished fact. Is it necessary to remind the Assembly of the various stages of the Ethiopian drama? For 20 years past, either as Heir Apparent, Regent of the Empire, or as Emperor, I have never ceased to use all my efforts to bring my country the benefits of civilization, and in particular to establish relations of good neighbourliness with adjacent powers. In particular I succeeded in concluding with Italy the Treaty of Friendship of 1928, which absolutely prohibited the resort, under any pretext whatsoever, to force of arms, substituting for force and pressure the conciliation and arbitration on which civilized nations have based international order. [Editor's note: A large section of the speech in which Haile Selassie discusses the political and military developments that lead up to Italy's invasion has been omitted.]

Forced to Mobilize

On October 3rd, 1935, the Italian troops invaded my territory. A few hours later only I decreed general mobilization. In my desire to maintain peace I had, following the example of a great country in Europe on the eve of the Great War, caused my troops to withdraw thirty kilometres so as to remove any pretext of provocation. War then took place in the atrocious conditions which I have laid before the Assembly. In that unequal struggle between a Government commanding more than forty-two million inhabitants, having at its disposal financial, industrial and technical means which enabled it to create unlimited quantities of the most death-dealing weapons, and, on the other hand, a small people of twelve million inhabitants, without arms, without resources, having on its side only the justice of its own cause and the promise of the League of Nations. What real assistance was given to Ethiopia by the fifty two nations who had declared the Rome Government guilty of a breach of the Covenant and had undertaken to prevent the triumph of the aggressor? Has each of the States Members, as it was its duty to do in virtue of its signature appended to Article 15 of the Covenant, considered the aggressor as having committed an act of war personally directed against itself? I had placed all my hopes in the execution of these undertakings. My confidence had been confirmed by the repeated declarations made in the Council to the effect that aggression must not be rewarded, and that force would end by being compelled to bow before right.

In December, 1935, the Council made it quite clear that its feelings were in harmony with those of hundreds of millions of people who, in all parts of the world, had protested against the proposal to dismember Ethiopia. It was constantly repeated that there was not merely a conflict between the Italian Government and the League of Nations, and that is why I personally refused all proposals to my personal advantage made to me by the Italian Government, if only I would betray my people and the Covenant of the League of Nations. I was defending the cause of all small peoples who are threatened with aggression.

What of Promises?

What have become of the promises made to me as long ago as October, 1935? I noted with grief, but without surprise that three Powers considered their undertakings under the Covenant as absolutely of no value. Their connections with Italy impelled them to refuse to take any measures whatsoever in order to stop Italian aggression. On the contrary, it was a profound disappointment to me to learn the attitude of a certain Government which, whilst ever protesting its scrupulous attachment to the Covenant, has tirelessly used all its efforts to prevent its observance. As soon as any measure which was likely to be rapidly effective was proposed, various pretexts were devised in order to postpone even consideration of the measure. Did the secret agreements of January, 1935, provide for this tireless obstruction? The Ethiopian Government never expected other Governments to shed their soldiers' blood to defend the Covenant when their own immediately personal interests were not at stake. Ethiopian warriors asked only for means to defend themselves. On many occasions I have asked for financial assistance for the purchase of arms. That assistance has been constantly refused me. What, then, in practice, is the meaning of Article 16 of the Covenant and of collective security?

The Ethiopian Government's use of the railway from Djibouti to Addis Ababa was in practice a hazardous regards transport of arms intended for the Ethiopian forces. At the present moment this is the chief, if not the only means of supply of the Italian armies of occupation. The rules of neutrality should have prohibited transports intended for Italian forces, but there is not even neutrality since Article 16 lays upon every State Member of the League the duty not to remain a neutral but to come to the aid not of the aggressor but of the victim of aggression. Has the Covenant been respected? Is it today being respected?

Finally a statement has just been made in their
Parliaments by the Governments of certain Powers, amongst
them the most influential members of the League of Nations,
that since the aggressor has succeeded in occupying a large
part of Ethiopian territory they propose not to continue the
application of any economic and financial measures that may
have been decided upon against the Italian Government.
These are the circumstances in which at the request of the
Argentine Government, the Assembly of the League of Nations
meets to consider the situation created by Italian aggression.
I assert that the problem submitted to the Assembly today is a
much wider one. It is not merely a question of the settlement
of Italian aggression.

League Threatened

It is collective security: it is the very existence of the League
of Nations. It is the confidence that each State is to place in
international treaties. It is the value of promises made to
small States that their integrity and their independence shall
be respected and ensured. It is the principle of the equality of
States on the one hand, or otherwise the obligation laid upon
small Powers to accept the bonds of vassalship. In a word, it
is international morality that is at stake. Have the signatures
appended to a Treaty value only in so far as the signatory
Powers have a personal, direct and immediate interest involved?
No subtlety can change the problem or shift the grounds of the
discussion. It is in all sincerity that I submit these considerations to the Assembly. At a time when my people are threatened

with extermination, when the support of the League may ward off the final blow, may I be allowed to speak with complete frankness, without reticence, in all directness such as is demanded by the rule of equality as between all States Members of the League?

Apart from the Kingdom of the Lord there is not on this earth any nation that is superior to any other. Should it happen that a strong Government finds it may with impunity destroy a weak people, then the hour strikes for that weak people to appeal to the League of Nations to give its judgment in all freedom. God and history will remember your judgment.

Assistance Refused

I have heard it asserted that the inadequate sanctions already applied have not achieved their object. At no time, and under no circumstances could sanctions that were intentionally inadequate, intentionally badly applied, stop an aggressor. This is not a case of the impossibility of stopping an aggressor but of the refusal to stop an aggressor. When Ethiopia requested and requests that she should be given financial assistance, was that a measure which it was impossible to apply whereas financial assistance of the League has been granted, even in times of peace, to two countries and exactly to two countries who have refused to apply sanctions against the aggressor? Faced by numerous violations by the Italian Government of all international treaties that prohibit resort to arms, and the use of barbarous methods of warfare, it is my painful duty to note that the initiative has today been taken with a view to raising sanctions. Does this initiative not mean in practice the abandonment of Ethiopia to the aggressor? On the very eve of the day when I was about to attempt a supreme effort in the defense of my people before this Assembly does not this initiative deprive Ethiopia of one of her last chances to succeed in obtaining the support and guarantee of States Members? Is that the guidance the League of Nations and each of the States Members are entitled to expect from the great Powers when they assert their right and their duty to guide the action of the League? Placed by the aggressor face to face with the accomplished fact, are States going to set up the terrible precedent of bowing before force?

Your Assembly will doubtless have laid before it proposals for the reform of the Covenant and for rendering more effective the guarantee of collective security. Is it the Covenant that needs reform? What undertakings can have any value if the will to keep them is lacking? It is international morality which is at stake and not the Articles of the Covenant. On behalf of the Ethiopian people, a member of the League of Nations, I request the Assembly to take all measures proper to ensure respect for the Covenant. I renew my protest against the violations of treaties of which the Ethiopian people have been the victim. I declare in the face of the whole world that the Emperor, the Government and the people of Ethiopia will not bow before force; that they maintain their claims that they will use all means in their power to ensure the triumph of right and the respect of the Covenant.

I ask the fifty-two nations, who have given the Ethiopian people a promise to help them in their resistance to the aggressor, what are they willing to do for Ethiopia? And the great Powers who have promised the guarantee of collective security to small States on whom weighs the threat that they may one day suffer the fate of Ethiopia, I ask what measures do you intend to take?

Representatives of the World, I have come to Geneva to discharge in your midst the most painful of the duties of the head of a State. What reply shall I have to take back to my people?

"I'll Go to Bed at Noon: A Soldier's Letter to His Sons"
By Stephen Haggard
From The Atlantic Monthly
1940

During the 1930s, a large peace movement resisted the re-arming of Europe. When Hitler attacked Poland in 1939 and war began, men who had sworn not to serve were faced with the reality of Nazi aggression. Men and women rushed to enlist in the military and in the war effort. The same pattern repeated in America after Japan attacked Pearl Harbor in December 1941.

Stephen Haggard was a successful actor in Britain. He had appeared often both on stage and in films. His father was British consul general in New York and was the grandnephew of writer H. Rider Haggard. When the war started, Haggard sent his two sons and his wife to America to keep them safe. Shortly before he joined the British army, he wrote an open letter to his sons that was published in The Atlantic Monthly. *His words again and again seem to predict his own*

death in the war. In 1943, Captain Stephen Haggard was
killed while serving in the Middle East.

———◻———

MY DEAREST SONS:

—I have just returned from Euston, from where I saw you
off this afternoon to America. You are both too young, thank
God, to realize quite what it can have meant to me and to
your mother to part as we have parted today. Britain is at
war, of course, and life is full of partings just now. You and
your mother are going to America to escape the possibility of
a wretched fate. You are not going, as people of the last century went, with ambition and high hopes; you are not even
going as the *Mayflower* pilgrims went, because they found
the way of life in their own country insupportable. If that
were the reason for your flight, there would be no great
tragedy in it. There would be wretchedness, danger, hunger
perhaps, the panic and the despair which fill all refugees
who are uprooted from the country and the people they have
loved for generations.

But you are fleeing because there is a chance—and on this
twenty-fourth day of June, 1940, a good chance—that all the
wisdom, all the kindness, the education, the comradeship,
the visionary development of the last fifty years, shall have
proved of no avail in the battle against evil which is now raging. I am not implying by this that the development of civilization in the last fifty years, especially in England, has been
well cultivated; but I do believe that never before in the history
of this globe have so many creatures so ardently and simulta-
neously desired peace, and worked to achieve it; and never

before has there been so blatant, cynical, and utterly inhuman a case of 'aggression' as Hitler's.

You will perhaps (and indeed I hope so) have forgotten, by the time you came to read this, what a frenzied German soldier is like, and the lengths to which he will go in order to rise to power—not power for good, but power for self-glorification and aggrandizement. I managed, in the twenty years between this war and the last during which I grew up, to get to know and to love the Germans—the people, I mean, not merely their music or their painting. I would not believe the men of the previous generation who fought in the 1914 war when they said the German was bestial. And yet I now find myself as venomous in my hatred of him as ever my father was.

However, it is not that which disgusts me so much; it is the fact that all the sacrifices of the 1914 war, the million of our best men, the shattering of the French countryside and of Flanders, their reconstruction afterwards, and the timid, ineffectual, and (I am beginning to feel) foolish groping towards a kindlier feeling between nations and a wider view of the destinies of the human race—all this has been wickedly and cruelly wasted, and I find myself, for the first time in my life, believing Hitler when he says that the Allies did not win the last war. Of course we didn't. We permitted the reoccupation of the Rhineland; we made all that sequence of tragic blunders ending in the most tragic one of all, the "peace" of Munich in 1938, which has landed us in a worse mess than ever the British people has had to face since the Dark Ages. It is because of that sequence of tragic blunders that you and your mother have had to leave for America today, while England is turned into an armed camp and I, an artist and a most pacific person, eagerly—yes, eagerly!—await the arrival of the little printed card which will ask me to report at such and such a place for military service.

Now I actually *want* to fight; and I believe that every man and woman in this or any other still-civilized country *ought* to fight. Your mother wants to fight too; but she is responsible for two tiny children, so I have begged her to leave England. That is her most effective way of doing battle. You will be three mouths less to feed, three less to be hurt in air raids, as your absence will mean that one house less will need to be inhabited. We shall no doubt need many, many children to repair the dreadful destruction which will presently be wrought, and I do not mean only the destruction of lives, but of all those things for which we have lived and are now to die. You are two of those children, and you will, I hope, be among the builders of the new world.

There *must* be a new world, for the only alternative now left to this little box of living space to which the radio and modern transport have reduced this globe is complete self-annihilation. Life groped its way to consciousness out of inert slime; and life will grow and develop again, if need be, from the smoking scrap iron and rubble of the last bombshell. And there is one advantage, too, in the widening of communications which the radio has brought about. Not merely evil but also good can speak across half the world to its own kind. The innate *desire* for good of the natural human heart seems likely to prevail in the end, and to spare some of us—you, perhaps—the doom of utter disintegration. At least I will hope so; this hope will enable me to fight, and indeed it is just this hope that I am fighting for. I have no hope for myself at all. I do not say this in despair. It is simply because I know and fear our adversary and because I refuse to underrate his strength. I do not see how we—that is, our forces as at present constituted—can possibly defeat him unless we work and fight and suffer a good deal harder than he. . . .

The air-raid warning has just sounded, It is the first time it has sounded since last September, and I had almost forgotten what the noise was like. I can hear the other members of the household coming down the stairs in their slippers to go into the shelter, I can't tell you how thankful I am that you're not home tonight. An air raid on London and two tiny children to be woken, dressed, and hustled down into a cold basement, there to await goodness knows what sort of fate! In the very far distance I can hear the thud of guns.

How soon, I wonder, will all these horrors be relegated to some shameful and unbelievable past? Will it happen in your time that bombers, sirens, and air-raid shelters will be fit only for museums or possibly as warnings to refractory and aggressive citizens? Will there come a time when you will be able to laugh at our pathetic attempts to fight a monster with fair words, and seventy-ton tanks with twenty-year old rifles? And if so, how will it be achieved? By annihilation of the Hitlers and the Mussolinis, or by complete surrender to them? I wish I knew. If I did, it would give me not only hope but strength to fight with. As it is, I am—we are all—fighting in the dark; and, while we wait in our cold basements for the bombs to fall, we ask ourselves what we can do—what we desire to do—to set the world to rights after the war. Perhaps it is up to us, who may not be alive, to hand on our knowledge, such as it is, to you; perhaps we ought to write down everything that we have learnt till now for the benefit of those of you who are still too young to learn, and who will be separated from us by the great gulf of this war. . . .

In this morning's post I find a little gray card which commands me to report at the Infantry Training Centre of the _____ Regiment by four o'clock on the afternoon of June 27. I had not expected it quite so soon. I had hoped to have about a week in which to tie up the loose ends of my untidy life. Now I have precisely forty-eight hours, for my train leaves London exactly forty-eight hours from this moment. For forty-eight hours longer I may continue my existence as myself; after that I must put away my individuality, my friends, my hopes, and my responsibilities and become the slave of a vast relentless war-machine. It is a willing, even a joyful immolation. But it is an immolation, a conscious sacrifice of all I have lived for up to now. I am not going with any feeling of exultation, nor have I any illusions about the gloriousness of war. My joy at going is caused simply by the feeling that I have stood too long shivering on the brink; and, as I told you, I like to jump into things with both feet: I prefer to take some decision even if it be the wrong one. And there is actually a certain satisfaction about this decision, for I have not taken it at all; it has been taken for me, and I am not responsible to my spirit for the possible evil results of it. . . .

It is broad daylight now. The town is awaking to life. I can hear the clatter of a dust cart a few streets away, and the hollow ringing of the emptied bins. One or two cars have roared up the hill.

I feel as if I were talking to two people who are separated from me by thick plate glass. You cannot hear what I am saying and so your faces are expressionless, though I can see you quite plainly and I have some sort of confidence that, sooner or later, you will hear the words I speak. But by then, alas! It may be too late for you to answer. You may shout as loud as you can—I shall not hear. Or, if I do hear, you will never know that I have heard. I wish I could believe in survival after death; but the only form of it that seems to me in the least credible is that form of "continuity of energy" which a piano wire will give off when it is struck, or the extent to which an electric wave will continue to vibrate after it has left the transmitter. Obviously if the blow on the wire or the energy behind the transmitter is a powerful one, the sound or the wave will continue to make itself felt for a long period; or if a human being has lived or loved or hated violently the vibrations that these strong feelings of his have set up may continue for a while, to be perceptible to people who are still alive, even though he himself may be dead. . . .

When you are confronted with an impossible task, ask yourselves always whether you are the first who has ever had to achieve it. Almost certainly you will not be. The records of our history go back nearly seven thousand years. In that time man's nature nor his elative circumstances have changed so very greatly. Almost certainly there will have been men or women before you who were faced with the same task and who had less certainty than you that it could be accomplished; yet they did accomplish it. So it should not be so hard for you

as it was for them, who came before you. You will have their
example. They had only their courage, and their faith in the
omnipotence of man.

For man is omnipotent. There is no goal he can imagine
in the realm of mind which he cannot reach sooner or later in
the realm of matter. There is no force yet discovered which is
strong enough to foil him: through his children he can overcome even the apparent finality of death. There is no fear so
potent that it will forever deter him, nor any suffering so great
that he cannot endure it for his spirit's sake. In him is every
quality that he attributes to his gods: beauty, wisdom, omnis-
cience, omnipotence, divinity. There is even immortality.

"A Plea for American Independence"
From a Radio Broadcast
By Colonel Charles Lindbergh
Mutual Radio Network, October 14, 1940

*War flared across the world in the years before the Pearl
Harbor attack yanked America into World War II. The debate
between isolationists who did not want America in the war
and so-called interventionists who supported greater aid to
Britain was loud. Charles A. Lindbergh was a national hero,
the first man to fly across the Atlantic. He was one of the
leading speakers for keeping America out of the war. The isolationist movement was led by the America First Committee.*

*He had visited Germany and had been favorably
impressed—as many American and European conservatives
had been—by the apparent success and vigor of Hitler's*

Germany. Hitler's virulent anti-Semitism did not concern most of the isolationists. Lindbergh was anti-Semitic himself, as were many leaders of the movement. It was a time when the hatred of Jews was widely accepted in America. After Japan's attack on the United States and the nation's entry into the war, Lindbergh and most of the isolationists worked to defend the country.

I come before you tonight to enter a plea for American independence. It is amazing that one should have to plead for American independence in a nation with a heritage such as ours; in a nation which in its infancy revolted against foreign control, and whose people have fought time and time again against the armies and interference of the Old World. Yet the independence and the destiny of America were never more in jeopardy than they are today. During the first century and a quarter of our existence as a free and independent people, we opposed, and opposed successfully, all the major powers of Europe. At the same time that our forefathers pushed through the wilderness to the Pacific, they forced, one after another, England, France, and Spain, to discontinue their interference with American affairs.

We won our independence from England when we were a nation of less than four million people. We numbered only ten million when the Monroe Doctrine was established. With a population of thirty-five million, even though we had just emerged from four years of civil war, we made France remove her invading armies from Mexico. Later in the century, with a population of seventy-five million, we forced Spain to withdraw entirely from the New World.

Why, then, with one hundred and thirty million people, are we being told that we must give up our independent position, that our frontiers lie in Europe, and that our destiny will be decided by European armies fighting upon European soil? What has happened to this nation that it fears in maturity the forces that it conquered in its youth? What change has come over us; what foreign influence has sprung up among us? Where is the blood of such leaders as Washington, Jefferson, and Lincoln; blood that stood firm on American soil against the threats, the armies, and the navies of the greatest empires on earth?

What we lack today is the type of leadership that made us a great nation; the type that turned adversity and hardship into virility and success. No one doubts that we are in the midst of a world crisis. No one denies that our defenses are weak, that our debt is great, that dissatisfaction is rising among us. We do not question the need for rearmament, for reform, for a better economic system. What we do question is the leadership that has brought these conditions upon us. We question that the men who were unable to foresee these conditions in time to avoid them, who could not foresee the war in time to prepare for it, who refused to believe the reports of rearming abroad when there was still time to take action, are now competent to carry this nation successfully through a period of great crisis. Under their leadership, we have alienated the most powerful military nations of both Europe and Asia, at a time when we ourselves are unprepared for action, and while the people of our nation are overwhelmingly opposed to war.

There is no question about the fundamental courage and solidarity of Americans when our national welfare is at stake. There is no division among us about the defense of our own country. We have always been ready to fight against the interference of foreign powers in our affairs. If need be we are ready to die for the independence of America, as our forefathers have died before us when necessity arose. On a clearly American issue we stand a united nation. It is only when we are asked to take part in the quarrels of foreign countries that we divide; only when we are asked to merge our destiny with that of other lands; only when an attempt is made to transfer loyalty for America to loyalty for some other nation.

The fact is today that we are divided; we have not confidence in our leaders. We have not confidence in their efficiency or in their judgment. Instead of a Washington warning us against the wiles of foreign influence and excessive partiality for any nation, we are told that our frontiers lie in Europe. Instead of a Lincoln telling us that if danger ever reaches us it must spring up amongst us, and that it cannot come from abroad, we are informed that we may be invaded from the ice-bound mountains of Greenland, and by fleets of non-existent trans-Atlantic bombers.

We find the same men who have led us to the greatest national debt in our history, now telling us that as a nation we are weak and unprepared; that we must appropriate more billions of dollars, and devote more years of time, to building up our military forces. These same leaders who have failed to solve even our peacetime problems, who have a consistent record of promise followed by failure, now ask us to put ourselves in their hands again as they lead us steadily toward that climax of all political failure—war. They do not tell us openly what their intentions are. They say we should leave our decisions and our destiny to specialists—to their particular specialists—to the same specialists who have made us a weakened nation in the center of an antagonistic world. They harangue us about "democracy," yet they leave us with less knowledge of the direction in which we are headed than if we were citizens of a "totalitarian" state. We are told that we are being prepared to defend America at the same time that orders are placed for the type and quantity of armament that would be used for a war in Europe.

We do not need untold thousands of military aircraft unless we intend to wage a war abroad. What we do need is a thoroughly modern and efficient Air Corps, trained, equipped, and maintained for the specific mission of American defense. What we need even more, however, is balanced action, a clear-cut plan, and a consistent attitude.

Adequate defense does not necessitate this alarm and confusion. With intelligent leadership, we could have built an impregnable defense for America without disturbing seriously our national life and industry. We have already spent more than enough money to have done this. With an army, a navy, and an air corps of high quality and reasonable size, we could have maintained our position with safety at home and respect abroad. But today, while we listen to talk of aircraft, guns, and battleships, couched in figures so astronomical that they compare only to our national debt, we find ourselves in confusion at home, and under ridicule abroad.

The same thing is happening to us that happened to England and France. We have been led to debt and weakness, and now we are being led toward war. Instead of building their own national strength, the peacetime leaders of England and France told their people that security lay abroad, that the best way to defend their own countries was to fight for Poland. They followed this advice and failed. Now we in America are being told under similar circumstances, and by leaders of similar caliber that our security lies abroad; that the best way to defend our own country is to defend England. All the lessons of Europe have passed unheeded before us. The effort that should have been devoted to the welfare of our own nation has been spread ineffectively over the difficulties of other parts of the world. The attention that should have been concentrated on the defense of America has been divided by a controversy over what part we should take in the wars of Europe.

If we desire strength, and freedom, and independence for our country, the first step must be to assure ourselves of leadership which is entirely and equivocally American. When a man is drafted to serve in the armed forces of our country, he has the right to know that his government has the independent destiny of America as its objective, and that he will not be sent to fight in the wars of a foreign land. The doctrine that we must enter the wars of Europe, in order to defend America, will be fatal to our nation if we follow it. When men are called upon to fight and to die for their country, there must not be even the remotest question of foreign influence involved.

If we desire the unity among our people that is essential to national life and strength, we must select leaders who believe sincerely in national defense, but who are wholeheartedly opposed to our involvement in foreign wars. Above all, we must select leaders whose promises we can trust, who know where they are taking us, and who tell us where we are going. Our vote next month can either bring or avoid a disastrous war for our country. We can either throw the world into chaos or lead it to new heights of civilization. The entire future of America and of our system of life hangs upon the action we take at that time. It does not depend upon the outcome of the war in Europe, but upon the quality and wisdom of the leadership that we choose for our nation in November—upon our Congress, upon our Senate, and upon our President; upon men, regardless of their party, who will lead us to strength and peace, rather than to weakness and to war.

CHAPTER THREE

Power, Authority, and Governance: Hate and Patriotism

A Review of the 1940 Edition of Adolf Hitler's Mein Kampf
By George Orwell
From The Collected Essays, Journals, and Letters of George Orwell: My Country Right or Left, 1940–1943
1968

George Orwell, whose real name was Eric Blair, was one of the best and most influential writers of the twentieth century. Orwell is most famous for his books Animal Farm *and* 1984. Animal Farm *is a sharp, funny satire of the Soviet Union in which the animals take over a farm and set up totalitarian rule under the pigs. Orwell warned of the danger of future totalitarianism in* 1984, *inventing many terms we still use to describe totalitarian rule. (For example, "Big Brother is watching.") Orwell opposed both Nazi Germany and Joseph Stalin's Soviet Union.*

In his review of The Totalitarian Enemy *by F. Borkenau, Orwell wrote about the nature of the Soviet and National Socialist (Nazi) regimes. Shortly before Hitler invaded Poland in 1939, he signed a non-aggression pact with Stalin. With the pact, Orwell wrote, "Suddenly the scum of the earth and the blood-stained butcher of the workers (for so they had described one another) were marching arm in arm, their friendship 'cemented in blood,' as Stalin cheerily expressed it. . . National Socialism is a form of Socialism, is emphatically revolutionary, does crush the property owner just as surely as it crushes the worker. The two regimes, having started from opposite ends, are rapidly evolving towards the same system—a form of oligarchical collectivism. "*

Orwell wrote extensively about the Nazis and politics. His review of Hitler's book, Mein Kampf *(My Struggle), was published six months after the start of the war in Europe.*

———□———

It is a sign of the speed at which events are moving that Hurst and Blackett's unexpurgated edition of *Mein Kampf*, published only a year ago, is edited from a pro-Hitler angle. The obvious intention of the translator's preface and notes is to tone down the book's ferocity and present Hitler in as kindly a light as possible. For at that date Hitler was still respectable. He had crushed the German labour movement, and for that the property-owning classes were willing to forgive him almost anything. Both Left and Right concurred in the very shallow notion that National Socialism was merely a version of Conservatism.

Then suddenly it turned out that Hitler was not respectable after all. As one result of this, Hurst and Blackett's edition was reissued in a new jacket explaining that all profits would be devoted to the Red Cross. Nevertheless, simply on the internal evidence of *Mein Kampf*, it is difficult to believe that any real change has taken place in Hitler's aims and opinions. When one compares his utterances of a year or so ago with those made fifteen years earlier, a thing that strikes one is the rigidity of his mind, the way in which his world-view doesn't develop. It is the fixed vision of a monomaniac and not likely to be much affected by the temporary maneuvers of power politics. Probably, in Hitler's own mind, the Russo-German Pact represents no more than an alteration of time-table. The plan laid down in *Mein Kampf* was to smash Russia first, with the implied intention of smashing England afterwards. Now, as it has turned out, England has got to be dealt with first, because Russia was the more easily bribed of the two. But Russia's turn will come when England is out of the picture—that, no doubt, is how Hitler sees it. Whether it will turn out that way is of course a different question.

Suppose that Hitler's programme could be put into effect. What he envisages, a hundred years hence, is a con-tinuous state of 250 million Germans with plenty of "living room" (i.e. stretching to Afghanistan or thereabouts), a hor-rible brainless empire in which, essentially, nothing ever happens except the training of young men for war and the endless breeding of fresh cannon-fodder. How was it that he was able to put this monstrous vision across? It is easy to say that at one stage of his career he was financed by the heavy industrialists, who saw in him the man who would smash the Socialists and Communists. They would not have backed him, however, if he had not talked a great movement into existence already. Again, the situation in Germany, with its seven million unemployed, was obviously favourable for demagogues. But Hitler could not have succeeded against his many rivals if it had not been for the attraction of his own personality, which one can feel even in the clumsy writing of *Mein Kampf*, and which is no doubt overwhelming when one hears his speeches. I should like to put it on record that I have never been able to dislike Hitler. Ever since he came to power—till then, like nearly everyone, I had been deceived into thinking that he did not matter—I have reflected that I would certainly kill him if I could get within reach of him, but that I could feel no personal animosity. The fact is that there is something deeply appealing about him. One feels it again when one sees his photographs—and I recommend especially the photograph at the beginning of Hurst and Blackett's edition, which shows Hitler in his early Brownshirt days. It is a pathetic, dog-like face, the face of a man suffering under intolerable wrongs. In a rather more manly way it reproduces the expression of innumerable pictures of Christ crucified, and there is little doubt that that is how Hitler sees himself. The initial, personal cause of his grievance against the universe can only be guessed at; but at any rate the grievance is there. He is the martyr, the victim, Prometheus chained to the rock, the self-sacrificing hero who fights single-handed against impossible odds. If he were killing a mouse he would know how to make it seem like a dragon. One feels, as with Napoleon, that he is fighting against destiny, that he can't win, and yet that he somehow deserves to. The attraction of such a pose is of course enormous; half the films that one sees turn upon some such theme.

Also he has grasped the falsity of the hedonistic attitude to life. Nearly all western thought since the last war, certainly all "progressive" thought, has assumed tacitly that human beings desire nothing beyond ease, security and avoidance of pain. In such a view of life there is no room, for instance, for patriotism and the military virtues. The Socialist who finds his children playing with soldiers is usually upset, but he is never able to think of a substitute for the tin soldiers; tin pacifists somehow won't do. Hitler, because in his own joyless mind he feels it with exceptional strength, knows that human beings don't only want comfort, safety, short working-hours, hygiene, birth-control and, in general, common sense; they also, at least intermittently, want struggle and self-sacrifice, not to mention drums, flags and loyalty-parades. However they may be as economic theories, Fascism and Nazism are psychologically far sounder than any hedonistic conception of life. The same is probably true of Stalin's militarised version of Socialism. All three of the great dictators have enhanced their power by imposing intolerable burdens on their peoples. Whereas Socialism, and even capitalism in a more grudging way, have said to people "I offer you a good time," Hitler has said to them "I offer you struggle, danger and death," and as a result a whole nation flings itself at his feet. Perhaps later on they will get sick of it and change their minds, as at the end of the last war. After a few years of slaughter and starvation "Greatest happiness of the greatest

number" is a good slogan, but at this moment "Better an end
with horror than a horror without end" is a winner. Now that
we are fighting against the man who coined it, we ought not
to underrate its emotional appeal.

Justice Robert Jackson, Dissenting Opinion in Korematsu v. United States
1944

*The Japanese attack on December 7, 1941, brought fear that
Japan would invade the Pacific Coast. Two months later,
President Franklin D. Roosevelt signed Executive Order
9066 authorizing the military to designate "military areas"
from which any and all persons might be excluded. The general in charge of the Pacific Coast designated the entire
region such a zone. Some 110,000 Japanese Americans were
sent to prison camps.*

*Fred Korematsu was an American citizen of Japanese
descent. He was convicted of remaining in a "military area"
from which Japanese had been excluded. The case reached the
U.S. Supreme Court, and on December 18, 1944, the majority
of the Court upheld the internment orders.*

*Three justices dissented, arguing that the internment
violated the Constitution. They were Frank Murphy, Owen J.
Roberts, and Robert H. Jackson. Justice Murphy called the
action the "legalization of racism." Justice Jackson, whose
dissent is printed below, later became America's chief prosecutor at the Nuremberg war crimes trials in Germany.*

Korematsu was born on our soil, of parents born in Japan. The Constitution makes him a citizen of the United States by nativity and a citizen of California by residence. No claim is made that he is not loyal to this country. There is no suggestion that apart from the matter involved here he is not law-abiding and well disposed. Korematsu, however, has been convicted of an act not commonly a crime. It consists merely of being present in the state whereof he is a citizen, near the place where he was born, and where all his life he has lived.

Even more unusual is the series of military orders which made this conduct a crime. They forbid such a one to remain, and they also forbid him to leave. They were so drawn that the only way Korematsu could avoid violation was to give himself up to the military authority. This meant submission to custody, examination, and transportation out of the territory, to be followed by indeterminate confinement in detention camps.

A citizen's presence in the locality, however, was made a crime only if his parents were of Japanese birth. Had Korematsu been one of four—the others being, say, a German alien enemy, an Italian alien enemy, and a citizen of American-born ancestors, convicted of treason but out on parole—only Korematsu's presence would have violated the order. The difference between their innocence and his crime would result, not from anything he did, said, or thought, different than they, but only in that he was born of different racial stock.

Now, if any fundamental assumption underlies our system, it is that guilt is personal and not inheritable. Even if all

of one's antecedents had been convicted of treason, the
Constitution forbids its penalties to be visited upon him, for it
provides that "no attainder of treason shall work corruption of
blood, or forfeiture except during the life of the person
attainted." But here is an attempt to make an otherwise inno-
cent act a crime merely because this prisoner is the son of parents as to whom he had no choice, and belongs to a race from
which there is no way to resign. If Congress in peace-time leg-
islation should enact such a criminal law, I should suppose
this Court would refuse to enforce it.

But the "law" which this prisoner is convicted of disre-
garding is not found in an act of Congress, but in a military
order. Neither the Act of Congress nor the Executive Order
of the President, nor both together, would afford a basis for
this conviction. It rests on the orders of General DeWitt. And
it is said that if the military commander had reasonable military grounds for promulgating the orders, they are constitutional and become law, and the Court is required to enforce
them. There are several reasons why I cannot subscribe to
this doctrine.

It would be impracticable and dangerous idealism to
expect or insist that each specific military command in an area
of probable operations will conform to conventional tests of
constitutionality. When an area is so beset that it must be put
under military control at all, the paramount consideration is
that its measures be successful, rather than legal. The armed
services must protect a society, not merely its Constitution.
The very essence of the military job is to marshal physical

force, to remove every obstacle to its effectiveness, to give it every strategic advantage. Defense measures will not, and often should not, be held within the limits that bind civil authority in peace. No court can require such a commander in such circumstances to act as a reasonable man; he may be unreasonably cautious and exacting. Perhaps he should be. But a commander in temporarily focusing the life of a community on defense is carrying out a military program; he is not making law in the sense the courts know the term. He issues orders, and they may have a certain authority as military commands, although they may be very bad as constitutional law.

But if we cannot confine military expedients by the Constitution, neither would I distort the Constitution to approve all that the military may deem expedient. That is what the Court appears to be doing, whether consciously or not. I cannot say, from any evidence before me, that the orders of General DeWitt were not reasonably expedient military precautions, nor could I say that they were. But even if they were permissible military procedures, I deny that it follows that they are constitutional. If, as the Court holds, it does follow, then we may as well say that any military order will be constitutional and have done with it.

The limitation under which courts always will labor in examining the necessity for a military order are illustrated by this case. How does the Court know that these orders have a reasonable basis in necessity? No evidence whatever on that subject has been taken by this or any other court. There is sharp controversy as to the credibility of the DeWitt report. So the Court, having no real evidence before it, has no choice but to accept General DeWitt's own unsworn, self-serving statement, untested by any cross-examination, that what he did was reasonable. And thus it will always be when courts try to look into the reasonableness of a military order.

In the very nature of things, military decisions are not susceptible of intelligent judicial appraisal. They do not pretend to rest on evidence, but are made on information that often would not be admissible and on assumptions that could not be proved. Information in support of an order could not be disclosed to courts without danger that it would reach the enemy. Neither can courts act on communications made in confidence. Hence courts can never have any real alternative to accepting the mere declaration of the authority that issued the order that it was reasonably necessary from a military viewpoint.

Much is said of the danger to liberty from the Army program for deporting and detaining these citizens of Japanese extraction. But a judicial construction of the due process clause that will sustain this order is a far more subtle blow to liberty than the promulgation of the order itself. A military order, however unconstitutional, is not apt to last longer than the military emergency. Even during that period a succeeding commander may revoke it all. But once a judicial opinion rationalizes such an order to show that it conforms to the Constitution, or rather rationalizes the Constitution to show that the Constitution sanctions such an order, the Court for all time has validated the principle of racial discrimination in criminal procedure and of transplanting American citizens. The principle then lies about like a loaded weapon ready for the hand of any authority that can bring forward a plausible claim of an urgent need. Every repetition imbeds that principle more deeply in our law and thinking and expands it to new purposes. All who observe the work of courts are familiar with what Judge Cardozo described as "the tendency of a principle to expand itself to the limit of its logic." A military commander may overstep the bounds of constitutionality, and it is an incident. But if we review and approve, that passing incident becomes the doctrine of the Constitution. There it has a generative power of its own, and all that it creates will be in its own image. Nothing better illustrates this danger than does the Court's opinion in this case.

It argues that we are bound to uphold the conviction of Korematsu because we upheld one in *Hirabayashi v. United States*, 320 U.S. 81, when we sustained these orders in so far as they applied a curfew requirement to a citizen of Japanese ancestry. I think we should learn something from that experience.

In that case we were urged to consider only the curfew feature, that being all that technically was involved, because it was the only count necessary to sustain Hirabayashi's conviction and sentence. We yielded, and the Chief Justice guarded the opinion as carefully as language will do. He said: "Our investigation here does not go beyond the inquiry whether, in the light of all the relevant circumstances preceding and attending their promulgation, the challenged orders and statute afforded a reasonable basis for the action taken in imposing the curfew." 320 U.S. at 101. "We decide only the issue as we have defined it—we decide only that the curfew order as applied, and at the time it was applied, was within the boundaries of the war power." 320 U.S. at 102. And again: "It is unnecessary to consider whether or to what extent such findings would support orders differing from the curfew order." 320 U.S. at 105. However, in spite of our limiting words we did validate a discrimination on the basis of ancestry for mild and temporary deprivation of liberty. Now the principle of racial discrimination is pushed from support of mild measures to very harsh ones, and from temporary deprivations to indeterminate ones. And the precedent which it is said requires us to do so is *Hirabayashi*. The Court is now saying that in *Hirabayashi* we did decide the very things we there said we were not deciding. Because we said that these citizens could be made to stay in their homes during the hours of dark, it is said we must require them to leave home entirely; and if that, we are told they may also be taken into custody for deportation; and if that, it is argued they may also be held for some undetermined time in detention camps. How far the principle of this case would be extended before plausible reasons would play out, I do not know.

I should hold that a civil court cannot be made to enforce an order which violates constitutional limitations even if it is a reasonable exercise of military authority. The courts can exercise only the judicial power, can apply only law, and must abide by the Constitution, or they cease to be civil courts and become instruments of military policy.

Of course the existence of a military power resting on force, so vagrant, so centralized, so necessarily heedless of the individual, is an inherent threat to liberty. But I would not lead people to rely on this Court for a review that seems to me wholly delusive. The military reasonableness of these orders can only be determined by military superiors. If the people ever let command of the war power fall into irresponsible and unscrupulous hands, the courts wield no power equal to its restraint. The chief restraint upon those who command the physical forces of the country, in the future as in the past, must be their responsibility to the political judgments of their contemporaries and to the moral judgments of history.

My duties as a justice as I see them do not require me to make a military judgment as to whether General DeWitt's evacuation and detention program was a reasonable military necessity. I do not suggest that the courts should have attempted to interfere with the Army in carrying out its task. But I do not think they may be asked to execute a military expedient that has no place in law under the Constitution. I would reverse the judgment and discharge the prisoner.

Hitler's Speech to the Commanders Before the German Attack on Poland
Obersalzberg, Germany, August 22, 1939

The most dynamic and charismatic leaders of World War II were Adolf Hitler and Winston Churchill. Although Hitler made many speeches directly to the German people, he also

*frequently delivered long, ranting speeches to his generals.
The war in Europe began when German troops smashed
across the border of Poland on September 1, 1939.*

*A week before the war started, Hitler spoke to his
commanders at Obersalzberg, his mountain retreat near the
town of Berchtesgarden in southern Germany. The text of
the speech was given to the British Embassy in Berlin by
American reporter Louis P. Lochner. For some twenty years,
Lochner was Associated Press bureau chief in Berlin.
Slightly different versions of the speech were found in
German records after the war and are part of the record of
the Nuremberg war trials.*

———▫———

No. 134: Letter from Sir G. Ogilvie-Forbes (Berlin) to Mr. Kirkpatrick

British Embassy, Berlin, August 25, 1939

The Ambassador has seen the enclosed which was commu-
nicated to me by Lochner of the Associated Press of
America. His informant is a Staff Officer who received it
from one of the Generals present at the meeting who is
alleged to have been horrified at what he heard and to have
hoped for the curbing of a maniac. Lochner specially asked
that his name should not be disclosed. It is interesting and
tallies in several details with information from other
sources. [Editor's note: Two paragraphs dealing with preparations to evacuate the embassy have been deleted.]

Enclosure in No. 314:
"Contents of Speech by the Führer to the Supreme Commanders and Commanding Generals on the Obersalzberg, August 22, 1939"

Decision to attack Poland was arrived at in spring. Originally there was fear that because of the political constellation we would have to strike at the same time against England, France, Russia and Poland. This risk too we should have had to take. Goring had demonstrated to us that his Four-Year Plan is a failure and that we are at the end of our strength, if we do not achieve victory in a coming war.

Since the autumn of 1938 and since I have realised that Japan will not go with us unconditionally and that Mussolini is endangered by that nitwit of a King and the treacherous scoundrel of a Crown Prince, I decided to go with Stalin. After all there are only three great statesmen in the world, Stalin, I and Mussolini. Mussolini is the weakest, for he has been able to break the power neither of the crown nor of the Church. Stalin and I are the only ones who visualise the future. So in a few weeks hence I shall stretch out my hand to Stalin at the common German-Russian frontier and with him undertake to re-distribute the world.

Our strength lies in our quickness and in our brutality; Genghis Khan has sent millions of women and children into death knowingly and with a light heart. History sees in him only the great founder of States. As to what the weak Western European civilisation asserts about me, that is of no account. I have given the command and I shall shoot everyone who utters one word of criticism, for the goal to be obtained in the war is not that of reaching certain lines but of physically demolishing the opponent. And so for the present only in the East I have put my death-head formations [Note from the British source: "The S.S. Death's Head formations were principally employed in peace-time in guarding concentration camps. With the S.S. Verfügungstruppen they formed the nucleus of the Waffen S.S."] in place with the command relentlessly and without compassion to send into death many women and children of Polish origin and language. Only thus we can gain the living space that we need. Who after all is today speaking about the destruction of the Armenians?

Colonel-General von Brauchitsch has promised me to bring the war against Poland to a close within a few weeks. Had he reported to me that he needs two years or even only one year, I should not have given the command to march and should have allied myself temporarily with England instead of Russia for we cannot conduct a long war. To be sure a new situation has arisen. I experienced those poor worms Daladier and Chamberlain in Munich. They will be too cowardly to attack. They won't go beyond a blockade. Against that we have our autarchy and the Russian raw materials.

Poland will be depopulated and settled with Germans. My pact with the Poles was merely conceived of as a gaining of time. As for the rest, gentlemen, the fate of Russia will be exactly the same as I am now going through with in the case of Poland. After Stalin's death—he is a very sick man—we will break the Soviet Union. Then there will begin the dawn of the German rule of the earth.

The little States cannot scare me. After Kemal's death Turkey is governed by 'cretins' and half idiots. Carol of Roumania is through and through the corrupt slave of his sexual instincts. The King of Belgium and the Nordic kings are soft jumping jacks who are dependent upon the good digestions of their over-eating and tired peoples.

We shall have to take into the bargain the defection of Japan. I save Japan a full year's time. The Emperor is a counterpart to the last Czar—weak, cowardly, undecided. May he become a victim of the revolution. My going together with Japan never was popular. We shall continue to create disturbances in the Far East and in Arabia. Let us think as "gentlemen" and let us see in these peoples at best lacquered half maniacs who are anxious to experience the whip.

The opportunity is as favourable as never before. I have but one worry, namely that Chamberlain or some other such pig of a fellow ('Saukerl') will come at the last moment with proposals or with ratting ('Umfall'). He will fly down the stairs, even if I shall personally have to trample on his belly in the eyes of the photographers.

No, it is too late for this. The attack upon and the destruction of Poland begins Saturday [Note from the original source: "August 26."] early. I shall let a few companies in Polish uniform attack in Upper Silesia or in the Protectorate. Whether the world believes it is quite indifferent ('Scheissegal'). The world believes only in success.

For you, gentlemen, fame and honour are beginning as they have not since centuries. Be hard, be without mercy, act more quickly and brutally than the others. The citizens of Western Europe must tremble with horror. That is the most human way of conducting a war. For it scares the others off.

The new method of conducting war corresponds to the new drawing of the frontiers. A war extending from Reval, Lublin, Kaschau to the mouth of the Danube. The rest will be given to the Russians. Ribbentrop has orders to make every offer and to accept every demand. In the West I reserve to myself the right to determine the strategically best line. Here one will be able to work with Protectorate regions, such as Holland, Belgium and French Lorraine.

And now, on to the enemy, in Warsaw we will celebrate our reunion.

[Editor's note: The following observation was added by the German officer who gave the document to the Associated Press.] The speech was received with enthusiasm. Göring jumped on a table, thanked blood-thirstily and made blood-thirsty promises. He danced like a wild man. The few that had misgivings remained quiet. (Here a line of the memorandum is missing in order no doubt to protect the source of information.) [Note from the British source: "This sentence in brackets forms part of the original transcript."]

During the meal which followed Hitler said he must act this year as he was not likely to live very long. His successor would be a hopeless one in two years at the moment.

"We Shall Fight on the Beaches"
Winston Churchill's speech to the House of Commons after Dunkirk
June 4, 1940

On May 10, 1940, Winston Churchill was named Great Britain's prime minister. The French and British armies had been driven back by the German army and were retreating. Three days after his appointment, Churchill made his first speech to Parliament, delivering one of his most famous lines, saying, "I have nothing to offer but blood, toil, tears and sweat."

The German advance continued. The British Expeditionary Force and elements of the French army retreated to a beachhead around the French town of Dunkirk. German panzers (tanks) under the command of several of the best generals of the war, Erwin Rommel and Heinz Guderian, hurled their armor against the Allies. Then, on May 26, Hitler made one of the great blunders of the war. He halted the panzers, saying that the German air force, the Luftwaffe, would destroy the enemy. But German bombs dug into the sand before exploding, and the Royal Air Force swarmed against the Luftwaffe. By the time Hitler allowed the panzers to attack again on May 28, it was too late. The Allies had used the two days to create defenses that held off the tanks. Over the next eight days, more than 228,000 British and 112,000 French and Belgian troops were evacuated. The British used Royal Navy ships, private yachts, fishing boats, and any other ship or boat they could sail to Dunkirk. While nearly all their *equipment was left behind, the men rescued at Dunkirk (and from other French beaches) formed the professional core of a rebuilt British army and of the Free French army.*

Churchill spoke to the House of Commons on June 4, 1940, to rally the nation and appeal for American help. [Editor's note: After discussing the campaign that ended with the evacuation at Dunkirk, Churchill talked about the dangers of a German invasion of England.]

——□——

. . . [O]ur thankfulness at the escape of our Army and so many men, whose loved ones have passed through an agonizing week, must not blind us to the fact that what has happened in France and Belgium is a colossal military disaster. The French Army has been weakened, the Belgian Army has been lost, a large part of those fortified lines upon which so much faith had been reposed is gone, many valuable mining districts and factories have passed into the enemy's possession, the whole of the Channel ports are in his hands, with all the tragic consequences that follow from that, and we must expect another blow to be struck almost immediately at us or at France. We are told that Herr Hitler has a plan for invading the British Isles. This has often been thought of before. When Napoleon lay at Boulogne for a year with his flat-bottomed boats and his Grand Army, he was told by someone, "There are bitter weeds in England." There are certainly a great many more of them since the British Expeditionary Force returned.

[Editor's note: Two paragraphs talking about war preparations in Britain have been omitted.] Turning once again, and this time more generally, to the question of invasion, I would observe that there has never been a period in all these long centuries of which we boast when an absolute guarantee against invasion, still less against serious raids, could have been given to our people. In the days of Napoleon the same wind which would have carried his transports across the Channel might have driven away the blockading fleet. There was always the chance, and it is that chance which has excited and befooled the imaginations of many Continental tyrants. Many are the tales that are told. We are assured that novel methods will be adopted, and when we see the originality of malice, the ingenuity of aggression, which our enemy displays, we may certainly prepare ourselves for every kind of novel stratagem and every kind of brutal and treacherous maneuver. I think that no idea is so outlandish that it should not be considered and viewed with a searching, but at the same time, I hope, with a steady eye. We must never forget the solid assurances of sea power and those which belong to air power if it can be locally exercised.

I have, myself, full confidence that if all do their duty, if nothing is neglected, and if the best arrangements are made, as they are being made, we shall prove ourselves once again able to defend our Island home, to ride out the storm of war, and to outlive the menace of tyranny, if necessary for years, if necessary alone. At any rate, that is what we are going to try to do. That is the resolve of His Majesty's Government—every man of them. That is the will of Parliament and the nation. The British Empire and the French Republic, linked together in their cause and in their need, will defend to the death their native soil, aiding each other like good comrades to the utmost of their strength. Even though large tracts of Europe and many old and famous States have fallen or may fall into the grip of the Gestapo and all the odious apparatus of Nazi rule, we shall not flag or fail. We shall go on to the end, we shall fight in France, we shall fight on the seas and oceans, we shall fight with growing confidence and growing strength in the air, we shall defend our Island, whatever the cost may be, we shall fight on the beaches, we shall fight on the landing grounds, we shall fight in the fields and in the streets, we shall fight in the hills; we shall never surrender, and even if, which I do not for a moment believe, this Island or a large part of it were subjugated and starving, then our Empire beyond the seas, armed and guarded by the British Fleet, would carry on the struggle, until, in God's good time, the New World, with all its power and might, steps forth to the rescue and the liberation of the old.

CHAPTER FOUR

INDIVIDUALS, GROUPS, AND INSTITUTIONS: PEOPLE IN WAR

Masters of Death: The SS-Einsatzgruppen and the Invention of the Holocaust
By Richard Rhodes
2002

Nazi power was built on hatred and an insane theory of German racial superiority. The Nazis, and most Germans who supported them, believed that anyone who was not German was inferior. The Jews and the Slavic peoples of eastern Europe were Untermenschen *(subhumans). They were to be exterminated to make room for German farms and cities. Hitler's anti-Semitism built upon a European and German anti-Semitism that had been growing increasingly brutal.*

The isolation of Jews was not enough. Hitler turned the SS (Schutzstaffel, or "Protective Echelon") loose in a rampage of mass murder. When the German army invaded Poland in 1939 and Russia in 1941 the SS Einsatzgruppen (or "deployment groups")—the killing squads—traveled with them. Death could be as simple as rounding up the Jews in a village and shooting them. Death could be as organized as it was outside of Kiev in the Ukraine at the gorge of Babi Yar. In two days, the SS and its Ukrainian allies shot to death 34,000 men, women, and children. At Babi Yar, the SS achieved a higher daily death count than was reached by any of the concentration camps. But the strain on even the SS was too high in the view of their chief, Reichsführer-SS Heinrich Himmler.

In part to save the SS from the strain of killing and in part to make the process more efficient, the Nazis built their death factories to industrialize and depersonalize murder. But before the gas chambers and crematoria of Auschwitz, Buchenwald, Dachau, and the other camps were created, the Einsatzgruppen and their allies killed.

Richard Rhodes's superbly researched book, Masters of Death: The SS-Einsatzgruppen and the Invention of the Holocaust, *details this lesser-known side of the Holocaust. The first selection gives an overview of the Holocaust. The second selection reports the reaction of Himmler to mass murder when he finally witnessed it himself and helps explain why the Nazis turned to the use of death camps. The third selection brings us to a small tragedy—but small only in the scale of death of the Holocaust—and the mass killing of children in the Ukraine.*

———□———

"Overview of the Holocaust"

The notorious gas chambers and crematoria of the death camps have come to typify the Holocaust, but in fact they were exceptional. The primary means of mass murder the

Nazis deployed during the Second World War was firearms and lethal privation. Shooting was not less efficient than gassing, as many historians have assumed. It was harder on the shooters' nerves, and the gas vans and chambers alleviated the burden. But shooting began earlier, continued throughout the war and produced far more victims if Slavs are counted, as they must be, as well as Jews. "The Nazi regime was the most genocidal the world has ever seen," writes sociologist Michael Mann. "During its short twelve years (overwhelmingly its last four) it killed approximately twenty million unarmed persons . . . Jews comprised only a third of the victims and their mass murder occurred well into the sequence. . . . Slavs, defined as *Untermenschen*, were the most numerous victims—3 million Poles, 7 million Soviet citizens and 3.3 million Soviet POWs." Even among Jewish victims, Daniel Goldhagen estimates, "somewhere between 40 and 50 percent" were killed "by means other than gassing, and more Germans were involved in these killings in a greater variety of contexts than in those carried out in the gas chambers."

So the Nazi hecatomb was not "modern" and "scientific," as it is frequently characterized, nor was it unique in human history. It was accomplished with the same simple equipment as the slaughters of European imperialism and, later, Asian and African civil war. State-sponsored massacre is a complex and recurring social epidemic. Understanding how its perpetrators learn to cope with its challenges is one important part of understanding how to prevent or limit further outbreaks, and no twentieth-century slaughter is better documented than the Third Reich's. . . .

"Himmler Views Death"
Lords of Life and Death

Heinrich Himmler personally attended a mass execution in
Minsk on 15 August 1941, at the end of the Pripet marshes
campaign. The previous day he and some of his staff had
flown in one of his command Junker 52S to Baranowicze to
meet Higher SS and Police Leader Bach-Zelewski and the
commander of the SS Cavalry Brigade, Hermann Fegelein.
From there the group, which included Himmler's handsome
chief of staff, Karl Wolff, traveled on to Minsk, where Himmler
spoke to the officers and NCOs of Nebe's Einsatzgruppe B.

After the speech, according to Bach-Zelewski, "Himmler
asked Nebe how many prisoners scheduled for execution he
had in custody at that moment. Nebe stated a number of
around one hundred. The *Reichsführer-SS* then asked if it
would cause any "special difficulties" if these prisoners were
executed the next morning. He wanted to observe such a liqui-
dation in order to get an idea of what it was like. He requested
that I accompany him together with *Gruppenführer* Wolff." Wolff
later claimed to know "from [Himmler's] own mouth" that the
Reichsführer-SS had never seen a man killed up to that time.
Himmler spent the night in Lenin House, one of the few public
buildings still standing in Minsk after Wehrmacht artillery
barrages and NKVD arson.

Otto Bradfisch's Einsatzkommando 8 and members of
Police Battalion 9 organized the executions the next morning
in a forest north of the city. Two pits had been dug in open
ground. Bach-Zelewski claimed in his postwar testimony that
"the criminals were without exception partisans and their

helpers, among which a third to a half were Jews," but Bradfisch testified to the contrary that "the shooting of the Jews was not a matter of destroying elements that represented a threat either to the fighting troops or to the pacification of the field of operations behind the lines; it was simply a matter of destroying Jews for the sake of destroying Jews." Of the victims, whose number Bradfisch estimated as between 120 and 190, two were women—still a new category of victims in mid-August.

Bradfisch claimed to have questioned Himmler before proceeding with the executions, asking him "who was taking responsibility for the mass extermination of the Jews. . . . Himmler answered me in a fairly sharp tone that these orders had come from Hitler as the supreme Fuhrer of the German government, and that they had the force of law."

The victims were held inside the forest and brought up to the pits by truck, one group at a time, to face a twelve-man firing squad. Wolff remembered them as "ragged forms, mostly young men." Bach Zelewski described an unforgettable confrontation between Himmler and one of the victims:

Among the Jews was a young man of perhaps twenty who was blond and blue-eyed. He was already standing in front of the rifle barrels when Himmler intervened. The barrels were lowered; Himmler approached the young man and asked several questions.

"Are you a Jew?"

"Yes."

"Are both your parents Jews?" "Yes."

"Do you have any ancestors who were not Jews?"

"No."

The *Reichsführer* stamped his foot and said: "Then even I can't help you."

Bach Zelewski's version of the massacre conflicts with Bradfisch's. Rather than a stand-up execution, Bradfisch described a *Sardinenpackung*: forcing the victims to lie face down in the pit and shooting down on them from above. Both Wolff and Bach-Zelewski remembered that Himmler was shaken by the murders. "Himmler was extremely nervous," Bach-Zelewski testified. "He couldn't stand still. His face was white as cheese, his eyes went wild and with each burst of gunfire he always looked at the ground."

When the two women were laid down to be murdered, Bach-Zelewski said, "the members of the firing squad lost their nerve" and shot badly; the two women were injured but "did not die immediately." Himmler panicked then. "*Reichsführer* Himmler jumped up and screamed at the squad commander: 'Don't torture these women! Fire! Hurry up and kill them!'"

Immediately after the massacre, Bach-Zelewski claimed, he challenged Himmler to reconsider ordering mass killings:

I said to him, "*Reichsführer*, that was only a hundred!"

"What do you mean by that?"

I answered: "Look at the men, how deeply shaken they are! Such men are finished for the rest of their lives! What kind of followers are we creating? Either neurotics or brutes!"

Himmler was visibly moved, Bach-Zelewski remembered, and impulsively called the men to assemble around him. The Higher SS and Police Leader paraphrases Himmler's speech, which he thought gave a good impression of his superior's "confusion":

Himmler first wanted to emphasize that he demanded from the men a "repugnant" performance of their duty. He would certainly not be pleased if German men enjoyed doing such work. But it should not disturb their consciences in the slightest, because they were soldiers who were supposed to carry out every order unquestioningly. . . . He alone bore the responsibility before God and the Fuhrer for that which had to happen.

They surely had noticed that even he was revolted by this bloody activity and had been aroused to the depth of his soul. But he too was obeying the highest law by doing his duty and he was acting from a deep understanding of the necessity of this operation. We should observe nature: everywhere there was war, not only among human beings, but also in the animal and plant worlds. Whatever did not want to fight was destroyed. . . . Primitive man said that the horse is good, but the bug is bad, or wheat is good but the thistle is bad. Humans characterize that which is useful to them as good, but that which is harmful as bad. Don't bugs, rats and other vermin have a purpose in life to fulfill? But we humans are correct when we defend ourselves against vermin.

The speech as Bach-Zelewski recalled it is hardly confused; it was a speech Himmler had delivered before and would deliver again. It incorporated arguments he had formulated that he hoped would relieve his men of whatever psychological stress they might feel at shooting unarmed victims: that they were only following orders; that the responsibility was not theirs but his and the Führer's; that any repugnance they felt was cause for congratulation, since it affirmed that they were civilized; that life at every level struggled for survival (an argument borrowed from Hitler, who had borrowed it in turn from the social Darwinists and the literature of colonialism); that their victims had purposes of their own and of course wished to live, not to die, but were harmful, were comparable to vermin.

But the experience of actually watching people shot down in cold blood was not something Himmler could so easily shrug off. After the executions he and his party inspected a prisoner-of-war camp. On the way to inspect what Bach-Zelewski calls "a small mental institution close by Minsk" they drove through the ghetto that Nebe had established in the Byelorussian capital, crowded by then with more than eighty thousand Jews. According to Bach-Zelewski, the hospital held "the most severe mental patients"; Himmler ordered Nebe to "release" them—that is, to have them murdered—as soon as possible. That raised the question of how to kill them. "Himmler said that today's event had brought him to the conclusion that death by shooting was certainly not the most humane. Nebe was to think about it and submit a report based on the information he collected." Bach-Zelewski claimed Nebe asked permission to try killing the patients with dynamite. He claimed that he and Wolff both objected, saying the patients were not mere guinea pigs, but Himmler ignored their objections and authorized the experiment.

The Reichsführer-SS spent another night in Lenin House, toured a museum the next day, flew over the Pripet marshes and Pinsk, then returned to Wolfschanze and shared his experiences with Hitler over lunch.

Himmler's panic at the sight of injured women, the firing squad's loss of nerve in the first place at the prospect of having to shoot them and Nebe's concern for his troops (but not for his victims) indicate the difficulties that the SS had to overcome to perpetrate mass murder on the Eastern front during the Second World War. Hitler's executioners may have been willing, but they were not always able. More difficulties emerged as the categories of victims enlarged to include women and children and, eventually, transports of western European Jews. Himmler's response to the Einsatzgruppe execution staged for his benefit in Minsk on 1 August 1941—his conclusion that death by shooting was certainly not the most humane—led directly to the development of more impersonal murder technologies; Nebe experimented that autumn not only with dynamite but also with carbon monoxide gas. . . .

The Children of Vinnitsa

In April 1942 the remaining Jews of Vinnitsa were assembled at the local stadium for a selection. Hitler would not occupy Werewolf until mid-July, but it was time to tidy up. Tailors, shoemakers, carpenters, builders and others with letter A work permits were directed to the left and returned to the micro-concentration camps adjacent to the factories where they worked: the rest—the elderly, women and children, perhaps five thousand people—were directed to the right. These were marched or trucked by the Ukrainian auxiliaries under German supervision to the commercial nursery north of town where ten thousand had been murdered seven months before. A long grave gaped open at the nursery with planks on

which to descend to the killing floor and a smiling German
officer to offer the ladies a hand down. A Ukrainian killer with
a machine gun sat on the rim dangling his feet into the pit,
smoking a cigarette.

But ten feet from the long killing pit the Germans had
opened a smaller, square pit perhaps twelve feet long and
wide. As they drove the groups of victims to the long pit, they
demanded the victims' children—leading the little ones,
pulling the babies from their mothers' arms, shouting, shov-
ing, beating, mothers screaming—and clubbed and shot the
children separately into the separate pit while making a
Sardinenpackung of the adults. Ukrainian historian Faina
Vinokurova was unable to explain why the Germans killed
the children separately at Vinnitsa, but two reasons suggest
themselves: to keep the *Sardinenpackung* tidy, lining up the
bodies of the adults; and, since children in their mothers'
arms were often shielded from the bullets that killed their
mothers, to make sure the little Jews were killed before the
pits were covered. In the same spirit, men from the
Einsatzkommando had visited the maternity hospital in
Vinnitsa that morning. New Jewish mothers and Jewish
women in labor had been carried away to the Pyatnychany
Forest and shot. The men had packed newborn Jewish babies
into two gunnysacks, like unwanted kittens, and thrown the
sacks out the second-floor window.

Himmler established field headquarters up the road in
Zhitomir to be near the Fuhrer. Goring built a bunker of his
own three miles from *Werwolf*, went about Vinnitsa in an open
car and supported the local ballet . . .

Notes from the Warsaw Ghetto: The Journal of Emmanuel Ringelblum
By Emmanuel Ringelblum
1958

The Jews of Poland faced several forms of hell from the Nazis. After their conquest of Poland in 1939, the Germans rounded up thousands of Jews from across the country and shipped them to the Jewish quarter of Warsaw, the Warsaw Ghetto. The ghetto covered about 1,000 acres (405 hectares), or 100 square city blocks. Normally, the district was home to about 160,000 people. Refugees and people forced into the ghetto ballooned the population to 400,000 by the end of 1940. The ghetto was declared a quarantine area and walled off from the rest of the city.

Jews had to wear white armbands with a yellow six-pointed star and were forced into labor brigades and worked to death. As the months passed, thousands starved to death. Up to 6,000 per week died of disease. Still more were beaten to death or shot. During 1942, more than 310,000 Jews were shipped from the ghetto to the death camps, most to Treblinka, where they were gassed. By April 1943, only about 40,000 people survived in the ghetto. They rose against the Nazis. It took the Germans four weeks to suppress the rebellion. Executions continued until the liberation of Warsaw.

Emmanuel Ringelblum led a small group of scribes and historians who documented the terrors of the Warsaw Ghetto. His journal is a vital narrative of life under inhuman conditions.

Ringelblum and his wife and young son were executed on March 7, 1944. His journal was found in the rubble of Warsaw after the war. (It had been smuggled out of the ghetto before the uprising.) Emmanuel Ringelblum's journal records life in the ghetto and the struggle to survive.

———□———

March 18, 1941: The Growing Number of Deaths

My dear:

The number of the dead in Warsaw is growing from day to day. Two weeks ago some two hundred Jews died. Last week (the beginning of March) there were more than four hundred deaths. The corpses are laid in mass graves, separated by boards. Most of the bodies, brought to the graveyard from the hospital, are buried naked. In the house I lived in, a father, mother, and son all died from hunger in the course of one day. Pinkiert, the King of the Dead, keeps opening new branches of his funeral parlors. He recently opened a branch on Smoeza Street, where he offers burial in "luxury" (i.e., for 12 zlotys, you can have pallbearers in uniform)—A scene: There's an apartment in a Jewish courtyard where traditional studies are secretly going on. The door of the apartment is opened only to the password (one knock). When you come in, you see a large group of Talmudic students sitting over their studies—Every day another attack on the Jews in the Polish newspaper for supposedly spreading typhus. Every day they repeat the warning to keep clean and avoid Jews—There's a new fashion for women—wearing kerchiefs instead of hats. The mode, in imitation of Christian styles, is flourishing . . .

August 1941: Lack of Resistance to the Nazis

A very interesting question is that of the passivity of the Jewish masses, who expire with no more than a slight sigh. Why are they all so quiet? Why does the father die, and the mother, and each of the children, without a single protest? Why haven't we done the things we threatened the world with a year ago—robbery and theft—those things whose threat forced the House Committees to buy up food for the poorer tenants? There are a great many possible answers to these questions. One is that the [German] occupation forces have so terrorized the Jewish populace that people are afraid to raise their heads. The fear that mass reprisals would be the reply to any outbreak from the hungry masses has forced the more sensitive elements into a passivity designed not to provoke any commotion in the Ghetto. Still another reason is that the more active element among the poor has settled down one way or another. Smuggling offers a means of livelihood for thousands of porters, who, beside the portage fee, take another 10 zlotys per load smuggled in to keep quiet. The shops and the orders from the German jobbers give employment to a large number of other factory workers and artisans. Some enterprising workers have turned to street peddling (bread, for instance, on which they make 25 groschen a kilo). The result is that it is the inert, unenterprising poor people who are dying in silence. Another factor in keeping the populace in check is the Jewish police who have learned how to beat up people, how to "keep order," how to send folk to work camps. Significantly, it is the refugees from the provinces who are dying of hunger, those who feel lost, helpless, in these alien surroundings. Their protest is converted into a beggarly cry of woe, an energetic demand from the passerby for alms, a protest of sorts to their own *landsmannshaften*, a demand for a piece of bread—from a Jewish institution or House Committee. However, the aid given them is not sufficient, especially when whole neighborhoods consist of nothing but poor people. And, after a few cries, they turn quiet, resign themselves to their fate and wait—in fact ask—for Death, the Resolver of all evil, to hurry. I had a talk with one refugee who had been hungry for a long time. All his thoughts were occupied with food. Everywhere he went, he dreamed of nothing but bread. He stopped at every store window where food was on display. But at the same time, he had grown apathetic, nothing mattered to him any more. It was hard for him to bring himself to wash, and he did so only because of his childhood training. Perhaps this physical passiveness, a direct result of hunger, is a factor in the silent, unprotesting wasting away of the Jewish populace . . .

Mid-September 1941: Smuggling of Goods into the Ghetto

Characteristic of the amount of smuggling in the Ghetto is the fact that several weeks ago (the early part of August, 1941) bread became dearer on the Other Side than it was in the Ghetto (i.e., so much bread was smuggled into the Ghetto from the Other Side that there was an actual shortage of it there). Most of the smuggling is during the early evening and after five o'clock, although there's smuggling at night too, particularly in certain places where the Wall runs through a courtyard, as on 5 and 7 Swientojerska Street. The same is true for Kozia Street. As a matter of fact, most of the smuggling there is via a gate on Nalewki Street, through which a German post wagon drives. The merchandise is immediately loaded onto rickshas and dispatched. Once a wagon drove up from the Frederik Fuls [soap factory] with contraband. There are Christian houses on Kozla Street with latticed windows. The Christians have bored holes under the windows, through which they pass large amounts of merchandise to the Jews. When they catch sight of Germans, they shout, "Joe's coming!" and the street empties out. Another smuggling route is via the hole connecting the former post-office building on Leszno Street with the finance-ministry building. The hole is regularly walled up by the Germans. But before the day is over the hole, the immortal hole, is open again. At 12 Ryrnarska Street, in the building that houses the Melody Palace, goods are smuggled across the adjacent rooftops. The man who makes the first approach to [a guard] and proposes that he go into smuggling is called a "musician" after the locale— Melody Palace. The guards don't take money; mostly they prefer "gifts," particularly gloves, socks, linen, etc. But they're not too proud to take money. However, money is taken as prepayment for a whole job, not for each wagon separately.

Mid-September 1941: Typhus Epidemic

Another subject, one which has been absorbing our attention for a long time, is that of the epidemic, particularly typhus. The doctors are fearful that next winter every fifth person—and some maintain that the figure will be as high as every other person—will be sick with typhus. All the disinfection techniques are of no avail. Instead of combatting typhus, the "sanitation columns" spread it, because they blackmail the homes where the rich live, where there really is no need for any disinfection, with the threat of ruining their linen, clothes, and the like. On the other hand, the filthy houses that really require disinfection are let off if the residents pay the columns. So the lice move freely all through the Ghetto. The overwhelming majority of typhus cases (some people maintain that there are about four or five thousand such) are concealed. The German health department speaks in terms of some 14,000 cases. The houses [where the typhus cases are concealed], are not disinfected; the lice carry the typhus from there all over Warsaw. The doctors are making a fortune out of treating people secretly, taking 50 and 100 zlotys for a visit. At the same time they decide in advance how many visits they will pay each day. It is worth mentioning at this point that the "sanitation columns" are so busy blackmailing the rich that they haven't the time to board up properly the windows of houses where typhus is discovered, to make them something like gas chambers; the result is that the lice survive and even increase.—The populace resorts to all kinds of measures to avoid the lice, but if one has to go through Karmelicka Street, which is crowded whichever way one turns, or through the bazaar at 40 Leszno Street, or through Walicow Street, or if one has to take the streetcar, or visit the public kitchen, one is bound to become infected sooner or later. The employees at the community institutions, such as the Joint Distribution Committee, or CENTOS children's aid, and particularly at TOZ medical aid, are particularly subject to infection. These officials have no money to have themselves inoculated (nor have the common people), and the serum is very expensive—one injection costs 400—500, and even as high as 600 zlotys. It is typical that all the serum comes from the hospitals of the Others or is imported from Wajgel's Institute in Lemberg. The cost is high, because in the first place the labor involved in making the serum is difficult (the internal parts of at least 150 lice have to be extracted by hand). In the second place, the serum has to pass through a number of hands, being contraband, and the price increases with each agent. People carry around all kinds of camphor and other noisome chemicals which are supposed to repel lice. Some people smear their bodies with lysol and other disinfectants. The poor people are not permitted to enter the houses of those who are better off, because they are carriers of lice. The disease has a mild course. Some 8 per cent of the patients die, many of them during the period of convalescence when a hearty diet is needed and the patients have no food.

The course of typhus is mild among the poor. On the other hand, for those better off there are often complications.

May 30, 1942: Nazi Murders

Last week was a bloody one. Almost every day saw smugglers shot. Particularly around the Small Ghetto, where a policeman who has been dubbed "Frankenstein" is on service. He was given this nickname because he looks and acts like the monster in the film of that name. He's a bloodthirsty dog who kills one or two smugglers every day. He just can't eat his breakfast until he has spilled the blood of a Jew.

Friday night, some eight or nine people were killed, a la Friday, the 18th of April. One of them was a man called Wilner (from 11 Mylna Street) who lay sick in bed. He could barely crawl out of bed at the command of the hangmen; he sat down on a chair, unable to move any further. So they threw him out of the second-floor window, together with the chair, shooting after him as he fell. In the same apartment three other men were shot (a brother-in-law of his called Rudnicki, his son, and another person). Reason unknown. Besides, three people from "the Thirteen's" Special Service were shot to death. This is all supposed to be a continuation of the clean-up of "the Thirteen." A few days ago, all Jews were informed via the House Committees that Gancwajch, Szternfeld, and both brothers Zachariajch were sought by the security police. Anyone found guilty of concealing them would be held fully responsible—together with all the residents of the house where he lived. Those shot to death yesterday (29th of May) include the notorious Judtowa. . . .

Last Letters from Stalingrad
Translated by Franz Schneider and Charles Gullans
1961

In the summer of 1942, a mighty German army crashed across the steppes of southern Russia. Following Hitler's

*orders, the army reached the city of Stalingrad (now
Volgograd) and the River Volga. The Russians fought house
to house to stop them. The German 6th Army was soon surrounded. Hitler refused to allow them to break free when they
still had the strength to do so.*

*Slowly, the army that had crushed Russian villages and
peasants as it advanced died. Some 300,000 German troops
had reached Stalingrad. Only 93,000 lived to surrender to
the Russians on February 2, 1943. A few thousand lived to
eventually be released after the war.*

*The letters in this section were on the last German
plane to fly out of Stalingrad. They were written by German
soldiers who knew they were soon to die or to be taken prisoners. The letters were seized by the German army. The
addresses to which the letters were to be sent and the names
of the writers were removed.*

*The men write about the certainty of death, about their
love for wives and children, and about stealing food to survive. One soldier, in a letter not included here, tells his wife
that she must marry again so their children will have a father.
Then he closes his letter, "Don't forget me too quickly."*

———■———

Letter # 5

This morning in the division command post, Hannes persuaded
me to write to you after all. For a whole week I have avoided
writing this letter; I kept thinking that uncertainty, painful
though it is, still keeps a glimmer of hope alive. I was the
same way in thinking about my own fate; every night I went
to sleep not knowing how the scales might tip—whether we

would get help here or would be destroyed. I didn't even try to come to any final conclusion, to resolve the doubt. Perhaps from cowardice. I might have been killed three times by now, but it would always have been suddenly, without my being prepared. Now things are different; since this morning I know how things stand; and since I feel freer this way, I want you also to be free from apprehension and uncertainty.

I was shocked when I saw the map. We are entirely alone, without help from outside. Hitler has left us in the lurch. If the airfield is still in our possession, this letter may still get out. Our position is to the north of the city. The men of my battery have some inkling of it, too, but they don't know it as clearly as I do. So this is what the end looks like. Hannes and I will not surrender; yesterday, after our infantry had retaken a position, I saw four men who had been taken prisoner by the Russians. No, we shall not go into captivity. When Stalingrad has fallen, you'll hear and read it. And then you'll know that I shall not come back.

Letter # 17

In Stalingrad, to put the question of God's existence means to deny it. I must tell you this, Father, and I feel doubly sorry for it. You have raised me, because I had no mother, and always kept God before my eyes and soul.

And I regret my words doubly, because they will be my last, and I won't be able to speak any other words afterwards which might reconcile you and make up for these.

You are a pastor, Father, and in one's last letter one says only what is true or what one believes might be true. I have searched for God in every crater, in every destroyed house, on every corner, in every friend, in my fox hole, and in the sky. God did not show Himself, even though my heart cried for Him. The houses were destroyed, the men as brave or as cowardly as myself, on earth there was hunger and murder, from the sky came bombs and fire, only God was not there. No, Father, there is no God. Again I write it and know that this is terrible and that I cannot make up for it ever. And if there should be a God, He is only with you in the hymnals and the prayers, in the pious sayings of the priests and pastors, in the ringing of the bells and the fragrance of incense, but not in Stalingrad.

Letter # 25

Just now the master sergeant told me that I cannot go home for Christmas. I told him that he has to keep his promises and he sent me to the captain. The captain told me that others had wanted to go on leave for Christmas too, and that they too had promised it to their relatives without being able to keep the promise. And so it wasn't his fault that we couldn't go. We should be glad that we were still alive, the captain said, and the long trip wouldn't be good in the cold winter anyhow.

    Dear Maria, you must not be angry now because I cannot come on leave. I often think of our house and our little Luise. I wonder if she can laugh already. Do you have a beautiful Christmas tree? We are supposed to get one also, if we don't move into other quarters. But I don't want to write too much about things here, otherwise you'll cry. I'll enclose a picture; I have a beard in it; it is already three months old and was taken in Kharkov by a friend. A lot of rumors are going around here, but I can't figure them out. Sometimes I am afraid we will not see each other again. Heiner from Krefeld told me that a man must not write this; it only frightens his relatives. But what if it's true!

Maria, dear Maria, I have only been beating around the bush. The master sergeant said that this would be the last mail because no more planes are leaving. I can't bring myself to lie. And now, nothing will probably ever come of my leave. If I could only see you just once more; how awful that is! When you light the candles, think of your father in Stalingrad.

Letter # 28

Even for me this letter is difficult, how much more difficult will it be for you! Unfortunately, there won't be any good news in this letter. And it hasn't been improved by my waiting ten days either. The situation has now become so bad we fear we'll soon be completely cut off from the outside. Just now we were assured that this mail will definitely get out. If I knew that there would be another opportunity, I would wait still longer. But that is just what I don't know; so, for better or for worse, I have to come out with it. For me the war is over.

I am in the field hospital in Gumrak, waiting to be transported home by plane. Although I am waiting with great longing, the date is always changed. That I will be coming home is a great joy for me and for you, my dear. But the condition in which I'll get home won't be any joy to you. I am in complete despair when I think of lying before you as a cripple. But you must know sometime that my legs were shot off.

I'll be quite honest in writing about it. The right leg is totally shattered and amputated below the knee. The left one is amputated in the thigh. The doctor thinks that with prosthesis I should be able to get around like a healthy man. The doctor is a good man and means well. I hope he is right. Now you know before you see me. Dear Elise, if I only knew what you are thinking. I have time all day long to think of nothing but that. Often my thoughts are with you. Sometimes I have also wished that I were dead, but that is a serious sin and one must not say such a thing.

Over eighty men are lying in this tent; but outside there are countless men. Through the tent you can hear their screaming and moaning, and no one can help them. Next to me lies a sergeant from Bromberg, shot through the groin. The doctor told him he would be returned home soon. But to the medic he said, "He won't last until evening. Let him lie there until then." The doctor is such a good man. On the other side, right next to me against the wall, lies a soldier from Breslau who has lost an arm and his nose, and he told me that he wouldn't need any more handkerchiefs. When I asked him what he would do if he had to cry, he answered me, "No one here, you and me included, will have a chance to cry any more. Soon others will be crying over us."

Letter # 32

Today, I talked to Hermann. He is south of the front, a few hundred yards from me. Not much is left of his regiment. But the son of baker B— is still with him. Hermann still had the letter in which you told us of Father's and Mother's death. I talked to him once more, for I am the elder brother, and I tried to console him, though I too am at the end of my rope. It is good that Father and Mother will not know that Hermann and I will never come home again. It is terribly hard that you will have to carry the burden of four dead people through your future life.

I wanted to be a theologian, Father wanted to have a house, and Hermann wanted to build fountains. Nothing worked out that way. You know yourself what the outlook is at home, and we know only too well what it is here. No, those things we planned certainly did not turn out the way we imagined. Our parents are buried under the ruins of their house, and we, though it may sound harsh, are buried with a few hundred or so men in a ravine in the southern part of the pocket. Soon these ravines will be full of snow.

From Those Devils in Baggy Pants
By Ross S. Carter
1951

The 82nd Airborne Division was one of the best units that fought in World War II. Ross Carter fought with the Division's 504th Parachute Regiment, landing in North Africa in May 1943 and fighting with the 504th in North Africa, Sicily, Italy, and finally in France and Germany after the D-Day landing of the Allies in France on June 6, 1944. Carter was one of only four men to fight from North Africa to the Elbe River in Germany. He was finally discharged in June

1945 after some of the most brutal fighting of World War II. In his preface to his book, Carter says, "My friends call me a refugee from the law of averages." In peacetime, his luck ran out. Ross Carter died of cancer in 1947.

Carter's account of his participation in the war, Those Devils in Baggy Pants, *was first published after his death. (The book has recently been republished in a trade paperback edition.) Carter concentrates on the enlisted men of the 504th. His fellow soldiers are identified by the nicknames they had been given in the unit or by pseudonyms. Thus, you will read of the Arab, Big Rodgers, Casey, and others. Carter often calls the 504th "the Legion." Writing about war, he also calls the Germans Krautheads. (Krautheads was a slang term used for the German enemy.) He also mentions being fired on by various German weapons. The enemy artillery is identified by its caliber in millimeters, resulting in talk of being fired on by a 75, 88, 105, 170, and others. The large cannon he calls Anzio Express—better known as Anzio Annie—was a 11.02-inch (280-millimeter) gun mounted on a railroad car. Annie could fire 550-pound (249-kilogram) shells up to 30 miles (48 kilometers).*

---□---

By the Banks of Il Duce's Canal

The 1st and 2nd Battalions of the Legion moved up to the high banks of the Mussolini Canal and there they stayed until sixty-three long, weary days had passed. The Krautheads sat up on the Alban Hills comfortably eating wieners and sauerkraut, peering through their top-quality range finders and spotting scopes, and at their leisure focused accurate fire at all points of the beachhead. We were surrounded on three sides, with the sea at our back. It was no unusual thing for artillery men to fire a barrage west, then north and finally swing their guns to fire due east. For the first time in the Italian war there were no safe back areas. The rear echeloners, who used to gloat because they had a gravy train, were under heavy fire day and night from the biggest caliber guns the Krautheads had: 150, 170, 210 and a larger caliber gun nicknamed the Anzio Express. The front line (where a man never felt safe) was about as safe as the beach. On our infrequent trips to the rear to take a shower we were always in a sweat to get back to the front line. We felt safer up there, where we had to endure only machine gun, machine pistol, rifle, mortar, small antitank gun, 75, 105, 88 and occasional 150 and 170 mm fire. Infantry on the front line offered targets that were too scattered to be worth throwing many extremely heavy shells.

The banks of the Mussolini Canal became the center of intense earth-moving operations. We tunneled holes that baffle description, and strangely enough we never did get through digging. A joker would dig five feet and be content until a mortar or 88 barrage tore holes all around. Then he would sink his hole down to six and after the next barrage to seven and so on till an artesian well stopped him. Finally he would drag up heavy timbers, cunningly erect a roof and shovel dirt on it.

We set up a platoon headquarters in one of a group of three houses which were about three hundred yards from the

Mussolini Canal. The squad leaders set up housekeeping in the other two. By day most of the men stayed in the houses, leaving a strong outpost to watch out for surprise assaults. Old gray-headed Duquesne, on approaching his house for the first time, inspected it with a critical eye. No prospective renter could have scrutinized its advantages or disadvantages more closely. He pounded his fist into the mattresses to see if they were soft; surveyed the burnable fences and doors; looked over the dairy herd like a discerning cattleman and then appointed competent chore boys to feed and milk them; gazed humid-eyed and moist-lipped at the flock of plump laying hens; searched and found tubs of lard and barrels of flour. Only then, these many things done, did provident Duquesne move his men in and take over.

Duquesne summoned an old peasant still living in the house to come to the henyard. Pulling his 45, he calmly shot the head off a fat hen and informed the stupefied old fellow that he wanted it for breakfast at eight next morning. Next he found three bushels of potatoes which had escaped detection on the first scrutiny and set his eager jokers to work peeling them for supper. Lovable Duquesne knew how to enjoy life and get the most out of any situation. But luck could be against him.

For example, while he was solemnly lecturing his satellites on the proper distribution of eggs, the correct manner in which to parboil an old hen, and instructing Sokal to feed the chickens, gather the eggs and guard against chicken thieves from other squads, a basket of eggs from 88's fell on the estate. When it was over, Sokal investigated and returned to report in a choked voice that a shell had landed

in the henyard and that but one solitary hen, with most of
her feathers blown off, had survived. Chicken feathers,
entrails, feet and heads were scattered over twenty square
yards. The old soldier's swearing was colossal, adequate,
and to the point. Tears flooded his eyes as he shook his fist
northward at the inconsiderate bastards who had wrecked
his poultry yard.

Casey and Big Rodgers carried a hind quarter of a cow
into the house which Winters bossed. Meekly and timidly
Rodgers explained that a shell had killed the cow and that
they hated to see good meat wasted. In a few seconds jokers
covered the bleeding carcass like jackals and in ten minutes
late-corners were scraping the bones. T. L. spent considerable
time cleaning his 45 that night. . . .

Replacements

Our front line outposts being as much as two hundred yards
apart, the Krautheads, armed with machine pistols, easily
passed through our lines at night and prowled unmolested for
hours. Our front positions were so well camouflaged that they
ran into them only by accident. If the two or three men on an
outpost detected a twenty-man patrol, they let them pass but
telephoned the information to a small reserve of tommy gun-
ners located back a few hundred yards, who would sally forth
to shoot it out.

It must have been very disconcerting and was certainly
misleading to the enemy to prowl behind our lines for an hour
and find nobody. When enemy patrols returned to their company
commander and reported that the line was weakly held, a

counterattack took place at the presumed weak spot. They came storming over almost every day and were always surprised when the boys rose out of their gopher-hole hiding places and scattered the ground with them. In a few weeks they held us in healthy respect. We captured a Krauthead once who complained about us in very flattering fashion, "We've got plenty of men and equipment," he said, "and we're full of fight and we don't mind tangling with most Americans, but you *verdammt* people are crazy. On that attack last week our patrols reported beforehand that only a handful held that line and we called on our artillery and then attacked. From somewhere you mowed us down and wiped us out by the scores. Our dead filled six ambulances. We don't mind fighting the regular infantry so much, but deliver us from those devils in baggy pants. You don't fight a fair war."

The shellfire competed with the rain in dependable frequency. We came to take both for granted. On waking up in the morning the Arab would look over at the Alban Hills and comment, "The bastards shelled us six times yesterday and the 1st Special Service Force on our right seventeen times. We are way behind and ought to get our share today." Or, "They poled in twenty-one separate barrages on our positions yesterday and slighted B Company, which got only nineteen. They'll even up the score today." Or, "They blew the roof off our house yesterday killing two men and three of our milk cows. Today they'll shell Gonzalez' house."

When we weren't being shelled or attacking or repelling attacks we watched the aerial activity over the beachhead, particularly the harbor. The 99th Negro Fighter

Squadron, known as the Flying Mustangs, had at that time some of the hottest pilots in the Mediterranean theater. We delighted in seeing them in operation. At night the enemy dropped long-burning brilliant parachute flares over the harbor. Night after night we watched the awesomely spectacular fireworks and shivered at the sight of burning planes falling to the earth or into the sea.

We felt naked and defenseless, with our lives dependent largely on luck. The soldiering skill which stood us in such good stead at Salerno, Volturno and Cassino could do little for us at Anzio. In one of his poems Victor Hugo describes the futile efforts of Cain to escape the accusing and punishing eye of the Creator. It was equally useless for us to try to hide from the evil eyes on the Alban Hills. . . .

We got many replacements, all fine boys with the strength of mules and the ignorance of old maids. We pitied the scared, bewildered, shy, eager youngsters who acted awestruck around us old boys. We felt sad when it became our duty to lead them into battle, because a large percentage of them got killed before they learned how to woo the narrow percentage of safety accorded by lady luck to discerning and sagacious warriors. They would die in the damnedest ways: One would trip over a mine and get a leg blown off; another would shoot himself or get shot accidentally; a third would let his foxhole cave in and smother him. And in the first battle they usually died in heaps. I must say though that those who didn't get it the first time wised up, husbanded their chances like the rest of us, and soon acquired the sixth sense so present, yet so intangible, in all veteran soldiers. Although the veterans died separately and not in bunches as replacements often did, they too would in time ride out the law of averages and go west in spite of the best of soldiering.

My platoon managed to find space in the house for its new men. Seven young replacements in another platoon, unable to find room in the house, had taken up residence in a strawstack in a shed covered with a straw roof. One day I strolled by, recognized the danger they were in, and advised them, since the ground was too marshy for trenches, to erect dirt-covered log bunkers on top of the ground as a shelter against flying shrapnel. Filled with the bravado born of ignorance, the youngsters didn't think the danger justified the trouble and continued to make coffee and be homesick. The next afternoon a mortar shell crashed through the thatched roof.

On hearing the explosion, we rushed out of our house and ran to them. They lay dying around the gasoline stove, their fourteen legs scattered all over the shed. Of all the gruesome images etched in my mental cells during 340 days of front line combat this was the most horrible and the most pathetic.

Later I went out to a strawstack adjoining the shed to get some stuffings for my bed. A stolid, solid, unimaginative trooper who was trying to match the amputated legs with the owner bodies, was engaging in a weird monologue which went as follows:

"Let's see now, this is a size eight boot for the right foot. Yeah, it fits him. Cut off at the same place. Here's his left foot. Now what about this blond kid? His leg is missing at the knee.

No, this'n don't fit I'll try this leg . . . no, it don't fit. Good, it matches. Hell, I can't find this guy's foot. Oh, it's under the straw. Well, that's a dam' good pair of boots to bury on a man. Poor devil, he deserves them though. One more kid now? Yeah, that's right."

As I listened to his stream of consciousness, I began to pull straw from the side of the stack. Something slippery and sticky came off it. Then I observed that blood clung to the straw in drops like rain to leaves and that the sunlight turned each drop into the likeness of a ruby. I got my straw elsewhere. . . .

CHAPTER FIVE

GLOBAL CONNECTIONS; THE THEATERS OF WAR

The Last Enemy: The Memoir of a Spitfire Pilot
By Richard Hillary
1997

Following Germany's rapid conquest of France, Hitler turned his attention toward Britain. To invade successfully, Germany had to control the English Channel and prevent the Royal Navy from sinking his invasion fleet. To control the channel, Germany first had to control the air. The Luftwaffe had to destroy the Royal Air Force (RAF) before it could attack the Royal Navy. The Battle of Britain was the Luftwaffe's attempt to destroy the RAF.

The Luftwaffe sent 1,300 medium bombers against Britain. (Germany had no heavy bombers.) To escort its bombers, the Luftwaffe had some 900 fighters. The best Luftwaffe fighter, the ME 109, could carry only enough fuel for eighty- or ninety-minute flights and that meant it could spend only about twenty minutes over British targets. The RAF started the battle with about 650 fighters, but throughout the period Britain produced far more new planes than did the Germans.

The battle started in late July 1940. By late August, RAF Fighter Command was close to being knocked out of the battle. Early in September, RAF bombers missed their intended military targets and bombed civilian areas of Berlin. In revenge, Hitler ordered Luftwaffe attacks shifted from Fighter Command to London. London suffered, but the RAF pilots had time to recover. The Battle of Britain was over. On October 12, Hitler canceled the invasion. Germany lost more than 1,700 aircraft while Britain lost about 900.

Richard Hillary flew Spitfire fighters for the RAF during the Battle of Britain. Hillary wrote his book, The Last Enemy, *when he was still only twenty-two. It came out in 1942. Hillary was shot down as the battle neared its end. He was horribly burned, and the last part of the book tells of his long recovery. He talked the RAF into letting him fly night fighters and died on a training mission in 1943.*

—— ◻ ——

Twenty-four of us flew south that tenth day of August 1940: of those twenty-four eight were to fly back.

We landed at Hornchurch at about seven o'clock to receive our first shock. Instead of one section there were four Squadrons at readiness; 603 Squadron were already in action. They started coming in about half an hour after we landed, smoke stains along the leading edges of the wings showing that all the guns had been fired. They had acquitted themselves well although caught at a disadvantage of height.

"You don't have to look for them," said Brian. "You have
to look for a way out."

From this flight Don MacDonald did not return.

At this time the Germans were sending over compara-
tively few bombers. They were making a determined attempt
to wipe out our entire Fighter Force, and from dawn till dusk
the sky was filled with Messerschmitt 109's and 110's.

Half a dozen of us always slept over at the Dispersal Hut
to be ready for a surprise enemy attack at dawn. This entailed
being up by four-thirty and by five o'clock having our
machines warmed up and the oxygen, sights, and ammunition
tested. The first Hun attack usually came over about breakfast-
time and from then until eight o'clock at night we were
almost continuously in the air. We ate when we could, baked
beans and bacon and eggs being sent over from the Mess.

On the morning after our arrival I walked over with
Peter Howes and Broody. Howes was at Hornchurch with
another Squadron and worried because he had as yet shot
nothing down. Every evening when we came into the Mess he
would ask us how many we had got and then go over miser-
ably to his room. His Squadron had had a number of losses
and was due for relief. If ever a man needed it, it was Howes.
Broody, on the other hand, was in a high state of excitement,
his sharp eager face grinning from ear to ear. We left Howes
at his Dispersal Hut and walked over to where our machines
were being warmed up. The voice of the controller came
unhurried over the loudspeaker, telling us to take off, and in a
few seconds we were running for our machines. I climbed into
the cockpit of my plane and felt an empty sensation of suspense

in the pit of my stomach. For one second time seemed to stand still and I stared blankly in front of me. I knew that that morning I was to kill for the first time. That I might be killed or in any way injured did not occur to me. Later, when we were losing pilots regularly, I did consider it in an abstract way when on the ground; but once in the air, never. I knew it could not happen to me. I suppose every pilot knows that, knows it cannot happen to him; even when he is taking off for the last time, when he will not return, he knows that he cannot be killed. I wondered idly what he was like, this man I would kill. Was he young, was he fat, would he die with the Fuhrer's name on his lips, or would he die alone, in that last moment conscious of himself as a man? I would never know. Then I was being strapped in, my mind automatically checking the controls, and we were off.

We ran into them at 18,000 feet, twenty yellow-nosed Messerschmitt 109's, about 500 feet above us. Our Squadron strength was eight, and as they came down on us we went into line astern and turned head on to them. Brian Carbury, who was leading the Section, dropped the nose of his machine, and I could almost feel the leading Nazi pilot push forward on his stick to bring his guns to bear. At the same moment Brian hauled hard back on his own control stick and led us over them in a steep climbing turn to the left. In two vital seconds they lost their advantage. I saw Brian let go a burst of fire at the leading plane, saw the pilot put his machine into a half roll, and knew that he was mine. Automatically, I kicked the rudder to the left to get him at right angles, turned the gunbutton to "Fire," and let go in a four-second burst with full deflection. He came right through my sights and I saw the tracer from all eight guns thud home. For a second he seemed to hang motionless; then a jet of red flame shot upwards and he spun out of sight.

For the next few minutes I was too busy looking after myself to think of anything, but when, after a short while, they turned and made off over the Channel, and we were ordered to our base, my mind began to work again.

It had happened.

My first emotion was one of satisfaction, satisfaction at a job adequately done, at the final logical conclusion of months of specialized training. And then I had a feeling of the essential rightness of it all. He was dead and I was alive; it could so easily have been the other way round; and that would somehow have been right too. I realized in that moment just how lucky a fighter pilot is. He has none of the personalized emotions of the soldier, handed a rifle and bayonet and told to charge. He does not even have to share the dangerous emotions of the bomber pilot who night after night must experience that childhood longing for smashing things. The fighter pilot's emotions are those of the duelist—cool, precise, impersonal. He is privileged to kill well. For if one must either kill or be killed, as now one must, it should, I feel, be done with dignity. Death should be given the setting it deserves; it should never be a pettiness; and for the fighter pilot it never can be.

From this flight Broody Benson did not return.

During that August-September period we were always so outnumbered that it was practically impossible, unless we were lucky enough to have the advantage of height, to deliver more than one Squadron attack. After a few seconds we always broke up, and the sky was a smoke trail of individual dog-fights. The result was that the Squadron would come home individually, machines landing one after the other at intervals of about two minutes. After an hour, Uncle George would make a check-up on who was missing. Often there would be a telephone-call from some pilot to say that he had made a forced landing at some other aerodrome, or in a field. But the telephone wasn't always so welcome. It would be a rescue squad announcing the number of a crashed machine; then Uncle George would check it, and cross another name off the list. At that time, the losing of pilots was somehow extremely impersonal; nobody, I think, felt any great emotion—there simply wasn't time for it.

After the hard lesson of the first two days, we became more canny and determined not to let ourselves be caught from above. We would fly on the reciprocal of the course given us by the controller until we got to 15,000 feet, and then fly back again, climbing all the time. By this means we usually saw the Huns coming in below us, and were in a perfect position to deliver a Squadron attack. If caught at a disadvantage, they would never stay to fight, but always turned straight back for the Channel. We arranged a system whereby two pilots always flew together—thus if one should follow a plane down the other stayed 500 feet or so above, to protect him from attack in the rear.

Often machines would come back to their base just long enough for the ground staff, who worked with beautiful speed, to refuel them and put in a new oxygen bottle and more ammunition before taking off again. Uncle George was shot down several times but always turned up unhurt; once we thought Rusty was gone for good, but he was back leading his flight the next day; one sergeant pilot in 'A' Flight was shot down four times, but he seemed to bear a charmed life.

The sun and the great height at which we flew often made it extremely difficult to pick out the enemy machines, but it was here that Sheep's experience on the moors of Scotland proved invaluable. He always led the guard section and always saw the Huns long before anyone else. For me the sun presented a major problem. We had dark lenses on our glasses, but I, as I have mentioned before, never wore mine. They gave me a feeling of claustrophobia. With spots on the wind-screen, spots before the eyes, and a couple of spots which might be Messerschmitts, blind spots on my goggles seemed too much of a good thing; I always slipped them up on to my forehead before going into action. For this and for not wearing gloves I paid a stiff price. . . .

That evening there was a terrific attack on Hornchurch and, for the first time since coming south, I saw some bombers. There were twelve Dornier 215's flying in close formation at about 12,000 feet, and headed back for France. I was on my way back to the aerodrome when I first sighted them about 5000 feet below me. I dived straight down in a quarter head-on attack. It seemed quite impossible to miss, and I pressed the button. Nothing happened; I had already fired all my ammunition. I could not turn back, so I put both my arms over my head and went straight through the formation, never thinking I'd get out of it unscratched. I landed on the aerodrome with the machine, quite serviceable, but a little draughty.

From this flight Bubble Waterston did not return.

And so August drew to a close with no slackening of pressure in the enemy offensive. Yet the Squadron showed no signs of strain, and I personally was content. This was what I had waited for, waited for nearly a year, and I was not disappointed. If I felt anything, it was a sensation of relief. We had little time to think, and each day brought new action. No one thought of the future: sufficient unto the day was the emotion thereof. At night one switched off one's mind like an electric light.

It was one week after Bubble went that I crashed into the North Sea.

From Iron Coffins: A Personal Account of the German U-boat Battles of World War II, 1st Edition
by Herbert A. Werner
1969

At a half-dozen major points, Hitler made decisions that ensured his defeat. One of the most important was to build a large surface navy. Building battleships and cruisers meant that Germany built fewer submarines.

When the war started, Germany had only fifty-six U-boats, or Unterseeboote *(submarines). Thirty of them, however, were small boats suitable only for the protected waters of the North Sea. As it was, in the first year of the war, the U-boats came close to isolating Britain. With enough of the large boats early on, U-boat commander Admiral Karl Dönitz might have won a German victory over England before America joined the war.*

The U-boats' window of opportunity was short. Soon, more escort ships protected the convoys, and ASDIC (an early form of echo sounding used to detect submarines), small aircraft carriers that sailed with the convoys, the entry of the United States into the war, and interception of U-boat communications eventually doomed the submarines. But during 1939, 1940, and much of 1941 they devastated British shipping. They remained dangerous throughout the war. By the end of the war, the toll was high. More than 780 U-boats were sunk or captured—93 percent of all German submarines that saw combat. The U-boats themselves sank more than 2,800 Allied merchant ships.

The selections here are from Iron Coffins, *written by former U-boat commander Herbert A. Werner. Werner fought as a U-boat officer from May 1941 to the end of the war. The first selection is from August 1941 when the U-boats were enjoying great success attacking British shipping. Werner was one of the few old-line U-boat captains to survive the war.*

—□—

We cruised the area for several days without hearing a sound or spotting a ship. Obviously the British had redirected their convoy traffic. The fruitless search began to affect the disposition of the crew. Paulssen, frustrated, contacted Admiral U-boats asking to be relocated into better hunting grounds. The answer suggested that Headquarters was receiving excellent intelligence from Nova Scotia: PROCEED UNTO AL 69. HALIFAX CONVOY EXPECTED GENERAL COURSE EAST-NORTHEAST ELEVEN KNOTS. LIGHT DEFENSE. GOOD HUNTING.

We raced westward at high speed for three days. When we arrived at our designated position it was night and the black sea breathed gently. U-557 stopped her engines, and the sound operator began his watch. However, we spent the night without spotting the enemy. With the first morning rays we resumed our chase and crossed the square in irregular patterns. At 1510 the same afternoon, as I was plotting course at the small table in the control room, a man on the bridge shouted, "Smoke cloud, bearing three hundred."

The Captain dashed past me and leaped to the top. I heard him hollering at the man in unmistakable anger, "You call that a smoke cloud? It's a forest fire! Crew on battle stations!"

When I reached my place on the bridge *U-557* had turned toward the black smudge. As we approached, the cloud expanded into a broad black curtain of dense smoke and fumes. Then we spotted the mast-heads and stacks of the zigzagging destroyers preceding the armada. Five minutes later a forest of masts crept over the sharp edge of the horizon. We were on collision course with a huge convoy.

1535: "Alarrrmmm!"

1545: The parade of ships had not yet appeared in the eye of the scope; Paulssen relied solely upon the report from the sound room. The crew moved quietly on action stations. The torpedo gang flooded the tubes. The second mate adjusted his computer. I took the helm.

1610: Two sweepers came into view, sailing in erratic patterns.

1625: The sound gear picked up two destroyers, propellers whirring at high revolutions. Both hunters made their moves as if not quite sure in which direction to search for the silent enemy. Asdic impulses began to bounce against our hull.

1635: The sound mounted in volume and density. The hammering of piston engines, the thrashing of propellers, and the knocking and rumbling of many approaching vessels reached a fierce crescendo.

1645: Wiesner had calculated the convoy's speed and course; the rest was up to Paulssen, and he swung his boat into attack position. His hands were busy adjusting the scope to the ups and downs of the sea, training the cross-hair on the fattest targets. Suddenly he shouted the decisive order: "Tubes one to five ready!"

"Tubes one to five are ready," assured Kern.

Paulssen released five shots within 25 seconds. We in the conning tower counted the seconds until the torpedoes hit. Meanwhile the Captain kept turning, extending and retracting scope, watching the cargo ships approach in orderly fashion. There they swayed in a sluggish sea, innocently carried away to their destruction. Within a minute this respectable parade of 45 rocking giants would be disrupted by fiery, breaking ships; the rest of the vessels would spurt away, their crews terrified by the horror of devastation.

Then came one—two—three hard explosions. The Captain, all smiles, shouted, "Exec, write down: hit on freighter, 5,000 tons; hit on second vessel, also 5,000 tons; hit on 4,000-ton freighter astern. Two misses. What's the matter with those damned torpedoes?"

1705: We in the tower were given a chance to view the holocaust. Three vessels lay heavily listing, shooting smoke and fire columns into the air. White lifeboats hung head down in their davits. Two destroyers raced toward the dying ships. It was a painting of rare and vivid colors.

1710: Depth charges detonated close by. Paulssen jokingly insisted that they were at least 1,000 meters away.

1720: Escorts disappeared. Sound contact with convoy was considerably reduced.

1800: Cook distributed coffee and battle sandwiches. Too much salami. The sweating torpedo gang hoisted up five steel fish and reloaded the tubes. The Chief balanced the boat like a juggler. The Captain sat at the scope watching the convoy flee toward the southern tip of Ireland

2125: *U-557* surfaced. Only a very thin light line in the west indicated that the day—a successful one for us—had come to an end. Darkness hindered our sight. But the convoy could not run away—we were too close to its heels. With both engines full ahead we pursued the battered herd.

2205: We signaled Headquarters: CONVOY GRID SQUARE AM 71. COURSE ONE-TWO-FIVE. SUNK THREE 14,000 TONS LIGHT DEFENSE.

Midnight: We turned to starboard and proceeded south. No convoy.

0030: We dived to sound out the depth. Reported the operator, "Propeller noise bearing three-oh-oh to three-six-oh, estimated distance ten miles." Ten minutes later, *U-557* surged back to the surface. Once again, the song of the engines together with the swishing noise of the sea rushing alongside the hull produced the hymn which accompanied us into battle. A flare fell in the east.

0115: Destroyer 3,000 meters on port. We drew a big loop around the escort, swinging into the convoy's wake. It was as if we drove into nowhere: sky and sea formed a solid black wall.

0220: Two escorts shot out of the darkness, showing their white mustaches.

"Alarrrmmm!" shouted Paulssen. "Dive to one hundred and seventy. Hard left rudder."

The furious commotion of our crash dive covered up the propeller noise of the destroyers, which were closing in on us with terrifying speed. We clung to pipes and equipment to hold our balance—that was how steeply U-557 hurtled into depth. Before the escorts could split her stern, she was already down to 90 meters.

Two charges erupted in our wake, flogging the boat like a gigantic whiplash. Total darkness enveloped us for long seconds. *U-557* fell and fell. It seemed to be the end. But the lights came on again, and Feder leveled the boat off at a depth of 200 meters.

0230: Both destroyers had stopped. Silence above, silence inside the hull. Our sound man reported other pro-pellers approaching. The escorts had called for reinforcement. We braced for a long barrage.

0245: One escort began to run up on our port side. We veered at high speed to avoid her spread. Then we heard three splashes, soon followed by three infernal explosions. The well-placed cluster slammed our boat deeper. Hydraulic oil spouted across the control room. The steel groaned, motor relays tripped, planes and rudders jammed, deck plates jumped. As the echo of the booms subsided, someone threw the relays hack in, the Chief reduced the speed to silent running, and all was again quiet inside the iron drum. The well-trained destroyer crews above had stopped for a new probe into depth.

0318: Another attack began: three cruel detonations came at close intervals. Then another run. We sat at our stations in the twilight of our emergency lighting, biting our lips and holding our breath as the Asdic pings grew unbearably loud. Some of the men lay on deck staring upward. Others were sitting and staring into an imaginary something. There was no talking, no coughing. The men showed no signs of desperation, only tiredness and stress. Hour after hour, the attacks were renewed sporadically and inaccurately. Depth was our prime advantage, our only protection.

1200: Above us they were still searching. The Captain ordered fruit conserves and biscuits distributed. A healthy decision. The men relaxed a little as they took on nourishment.

1412: The latest barrage brought to 128 the number of canisters dropped upon us. But the soundman claimed that he heard two escorts leave the scene. We were hopeful.

1520: Not a single detonation for over one hour. Had the Tommies run out of depth charges? Had they abandoned their game? The sound operator turned his wheel with loving care. The entire horizon seemed to be free of hostile sound. Where was the third hunter?

Paulssen said, "Start up bilge pump, let's see whether they take that bait."

The impertinent grinding sound tortured us like a dentist's drill. Though it betrayed our position, it produced no response from above. The third enemy had also departed.

1610: *U-557* surfaced after being submerged for 14 hours. As the Captain opened the bridge hatch, I was literally thrown out of the hull by our internal pressure. Brilliant weather greeted us; we inhaled the fresh air gratefully, though a sudden abundance of it almost made us black out. The ventilators transported oxygen to the sweating hands inside the drum. For us on the bridge, the sun was never so red nor the sky so blue. Since the convoy had fled safely beyond our reach, *U-557* raced west in search of new targets. . . .

On the second day of Christmas, the earth began to tremble and there was a steady rumbling in the distance. I knew the sound well: it meant that a city was being bombed into dust—in this case, Hamburg. I took my powerful binoculars and posted myself on the nearby highway which commanded an excellent view of the countryside.

The sky was pale blue and cloudless, the air cold and clear. A white winter sun shone over Hamburg, and from where I stood I could see the glint of the sun on the wings and fuselages of Flying Fortresses coming in from the sea. They glided out of the sky and moved relentlessly forward. Flight after flight pushed through the haze in the distance and droned over the dying city. Tiny gray and black flak clouds popped up among the hundreds of bombers and their countless fighter escorts. Through my glasses I saw the bombs raining down upon Hamburg, aircraft exploding, red and yellow fireballs erupting in the silken sky, burning planes tumbling through the air, our Messerschmitt fighters plunging upon the bombers like hawks, filling the sky with debris. The ground shook under my feet, many kilometers away from the target. Thousands of innocents, who had prayed on Christmas Eve, were being roasted alive and turned into ashes. And I thought that my loved ones must have died the same way.

What a miserable, obscene war, where able-bodied men and sophisticated machines were employed to exterminate the helpless and harmless. I told myself that my war was quite a different kind of struggle, that it was a war in which ships were engaged to sink ships, weapons, and supplies before they could be used to destroy. But whichever way one fought the war, the total results were indivisible and hideous beyond the powers of men to comprehend. Death on a gigantic scale had become so routine that life itself seemed rather odd and irrelevant, and all the once-commonplace joys of life seemed abnormal, ludicrous and weird. Even the love of a generous woman came as an unreal interruption in the normal nightmare of survival.

From Brave Men
By Ernie Pyle
1944

If you want to truly understand the fighting in World War II, read Ernie Pyle. Read Brave Men, Here Is Your War, Last

Chapter, *or read the 1986 anthology of his articles,* Ernie's War. *Ernie Pyle's words are simple, direct, and powerful.*

Pyle was probably the best war correspondent of World War II. He wrote little about generals and their grand tactics and strategies. Pyle wrote about the average GI, the guys who slept in foxholes in the mud and rain of Normandy. He wrote about the soldiers who fought the long, hard battles in the mountains of Italy. Ernie Pyle moved with the troops as they landed in North Africa in 1942. He told their stories as they fought through the campaigns in Sicily, Italy, and France.

From Italy, he told of the bodies of the dead, slung belly-down over the backs of mules, to be carried down the steep mountains. One of the bodies was that of a young captain who was liked and respected by his men. As the body lay on the ground, a soldier came over, and took the dead captain's hand. The man sat in silence for "a full five minutes."

"Finally he put the hand down. He reached over and gently straightened the points of the captain's shirt collar, and then he sort of rearranged the tattered edges of the uniform around the wound, and then he got up and walked away down the road in the moonlight, all alone.

"The rest of us went back into the cowshed, leaving the five dead men lying in a line end to end in the shadow of the low stone wall. We lay down on the straw in the cowshed, and pretty soon we were all asleep."

Ernie Pyle landed at Normandy the day after D-Day and walked the beach strewn with the debris of war. He wrote of the writing paper and envelopes men carried, men who had died on the coast of France, and "the letters—now forever incapable of being written—that might have filled those blank abandoned pages!" He wrote of the movement of war: "Over and around this long thin line of personal anguish, fresh men were rushing vast supplies to keep our armies pushing on into France."

Ernie Pyle survived the war in Europe. Rather than go home, which he should have done, he went to the Pacific to report on the end of the war against Japan. He was killed by Japanese machine-gun fire during the Okinawa campaign in 1945.

The first selection is from the 1943 campaign on the Italian island of Sicily. Pyle became ill and was kept in a field hospital. He tells of the fight by the doctors to save lives and of their successes. In this selection, he tells of the death of one man.

The second selection reports on the campaign on the Cherbourg Peninsula after the D-Day landing. Breaking out of the beachheads, the Allied troops fought a slow, hard battle across the fields and villages of France.

———□———

DEATH IN A HOSPITAL

Dying men were brought into our tent, men whose death rattle silenced the conversation and made all of us thoughtful. When a man was almost gone, the surgeons would put a piece of gauze over his face. He could breathe through it but we couldn't see his face well.

Twice within five minutes chaplains came running. One of those occasions haunted me for hours. The wounded man was still semiconscious. The chaplain knelt down beside him and two wardboys squatted nearby. The chaplain said, "John, I'm going to say a prayer for you."

Somehow this stark announcement hit me like a hammer. He didn't say, "I'm going to pray for you to get well," he just said he was going to say a prayer, and it was obvious to me that he meant the final prayer. It was as though he had said, "Brother, you may not know it, but your goose is cooked." Anyhow, he voiced the prayer, and the weak, gasping man tried vainly to repeat the words after him. When he had finished, the chaplain added, "John, you're doing fine, you're doing fine." Then he rose and dashed off on some other call, and the wardboys went about their duties.

The dying man was left utterly alone, just lying there on his litter on the ground, lying in an aisle, because the tent was full. Of course it couldn't be otherwise, but the aloneness of that man as he went through the last few minutes of his life was what tormented me. I felt like going over and at least holding his hand while he died, but it would have been out of order and I didn't do it. I wish now I had.

HEDGEROW FIGHTING

I want to describe to you what the weird hedgerow fighting in northwestern France was like. This type of fighting was always in small groups, so let's take as an example one company of men. Let's say they were working forward on both sides of a country lane, and the company was responsible for clearing the two fields on either side of the road as it advanced. That meant there was only about one platoon to a field, and with the company's under-strength from casualties, there might be no more than twenty-five or thirty men.

The fields were usually not more than fifty yards across and a couple of hundred yards long. They might have grain in them, or apple trees, but mostly they were just pastures of green grass, full of beautiful cows. The fields were surrounded on all sides by the immense hedgerows—ancient earthen banks, waist high, all matted with roots, and out of which grew weeds, bushes, and trees up to twenty feet high. The Germans used these barriers well. They put snipers in the trees. They dug deep trenches behind the hedgerows and covered them with timber, so that it was almost impossible for artillery to get at them. Sometimes they propped up machine guns with strings attached so that they could fire over the hedge without getting out of their holes. They even cut out a section of the hedgerow and hid a big gun or a tank in it, covering it with bush. Also they tunneled under the hedgerows from the back and made the opening on the forward side just large enough to stick a machine gun through. But mostly the hedgerow pattern was this: a heavy machine gun hidden at each end of the field and infantrymen hidden all along the hedgerow with rifles and machine pistols.

We had to dig them out. It was a slow and cautious business, and there was nothing dashing about it. Our men didn't go across the open fields in dramatic charges such as you see in the movies. They did at first, but they learned better. They went in tiny groups, a squad or less, moving yards apart and sticking close to the hedgerows on either end of the field. They crept a few yards, squatted, waited, then crept again.

If you could have been right up there between the Germans and the Americans you wouldn't have seen many men at any one time—just a few here and there, always trying to keep hidden. But you would have heard an awful lot of noise. Our men were taught in training not to fire until they saw something to fire at. But the principle didn't work in that country, because there was very little to see. So the alternative was to keep shooting constantly at the hedgerows. That pinned the Germans to their holes while we sneaked up on them. The attacking squads sneaked up the sides of the hedgerows while the rest of the platoon stayed back in their own hedgerow and kept the forward hedge saturated with bullets. They shot rifle grenades too, and a mortar squad a little farther back kept lobbing mortar shells over onto the Germans. The little advance groups worked their way up to the far ends of the hedgerows at the corners of the field. They first tried to knock out the machine guns at each corner. They did this with hand grenades, rifle grenades and machine guns.

Usually, when the pressure was on, the German defenders of the hedgerow started pulling back. They would take their heavier guns and most of the men back a couple of fields and start digging in for a new line. They left about two machine guns and a few riflemen scattered through the hedge to do a lot of shooting and hold up the Americans as long as they could. Our men would then sneak along the front side of the hedgerow, throwing grenades over onto the other side and spraying the hedges with their guns. The fighting was close—only a few yards apart—but it was seldom actual hand-to-hand stuff. Sometimes the remaining Germans came out of their holes with their hands up. Sometimes they tried to run for it and were mowed down. Sometimes they wouldn't come out at all, and a hand grenade, thrown into their hole, finished them off. And so another hedgerow was taken and we were ready to start on the one beyond.

This hedgerow business was a series of little skirmishes like that clear across the front, thousands and thousands of little skirmishes. No single one of them was very big. Added up over the days and weeks, however, they made a man-sized war—with thousands on both sides getting killed. But that is only a general pattern of the hedgerow fighting. Actually each one was a little separate war, fought under different circumstances. For instance, the fight might be in a woods instead of an open field. The Germans would be dug in all over the woods, in little groups, and it was really tough to get them out. Often in cases like that we just went around the woods and kept going, and let later units take care of those surrounded and doomed fellows. Or we might go through a woods and clean it out, and another company, coming through a couple of hours later, would find it full of Germans again. In a war like this everything was in such confusion that I never could see how either side ever got anywhere.

Sometimes we didn't know where the enemy was and didn't know where our own troops were. As somebody said one day, no battalion commander could have given you the exact location of his various units five minutes after they had jumped off. Gradually the front got all mixed up. There were Germans behind us and at the side. They would be shooting at us from behind and from our flank. Sometimes a unit got so far out ahead of those on either side that it had to swing around and fight to its rear. Sometimes we fired on our own troops, thinking we were in German territory. It was hard to see anything, or even tell from the sounds, for each side used some of the other's captured weapons.

The tanks and the infantry had to work in the closest cooperation in breaking through the German ring that tried to pin us down in the beachhead area. Neither could have done it alone. The troops were of two minds about having tanks around them. If you're a foot soldier you hate to be near a tank, for it always draws fire. On the other hand, if the going gets tough you pray for a tank to come up and start blasting with its guns. In our break-through each infantry unit had tanks attached to it. It was the tanks and the infantry that broke through that ring and punched a hole for the armored divisions to follow after. The armored divisions practically ran amuck, racing long distances and playing hob, once they got behind the German lines, but it was the infantry and their attached tanks that opened the gate for them. Tanks shuttled back and forth, from one field to another, throughout our break-through battle, receiving their orders by radio. Bulldozers punched holes through the hedgerows for them, and then the tanks would come up and blast out the bad spots of the opposition.

It was necessary for us to wreck almost every farm-house and little village in our path. The Germans used them for strong points or put artillery observers in them, and they just had to be blasted out. Most of the French farmers evacuated ahead of the fighting and filtered back after it had passed. It was pitiful to see them come back to their demolished homes and towns. Yet it was wonderful to see the grand way they took it.

In a long drive an infantry company often went for a couple of days without letting up. Ammunition was carried up to it by hand, and occasionally by jeep. The soldiers sometimes ate only one K ration a day. They sometimes ran out of water. Their strength was gradually whittled down by wounds, exhaustion cases and straggling. Finally they would get an order to sit where they were and dig in. Then another company would pass through, or around them, and go on with the fighting. The relieved company might get to rest as much as a day or two. But in a big push such as the one that broke us out of the beach-head, a few hours' respite was about all they could expect.

The company I was with got its orders to rest about five o'clock one afternoon. They dug foxholes along the hedgerows, or commandeered German ones already dug. Regardless of how tired a man might be, he always dug in the first thing. Then they sent some men looking for water. They got more K rations up by jeep, and sat on the ground eating them. They hoped they would stay there all night, but they weren't counting on it too much. Shortly after supper a lieutenant came out of a farmhouse and told the sergeants to pass the word to be ready to move in ten minutes. They bundled on their packs and started just before dark. Within half an hour they had run into a new fight that lasted all night. They had had less than four hours' rest in three solid days of fighting . . .

The Ayers Report on the decision to drop the Atomic bomb
Date unknown

After observing the first test of the atomic bomb, lead scientist Robert Oppenheimer recalled a line of Hindu scripture, "Now I am become Death, the destroyer of worlds."

On August 6, 1945, a single American B-29 bomber dropped a single bomb on the Japanese city of Hiroshima. Three days later, another bomb destroyed Nagasaki. In looking at the dropping of the two bombs, we must remember the context of the decisions and the expectations of America's leaders.

By the end of the war, the art of death had reached a previously unimaginable level, and conventional bombing could be as deadly as the small atomic bombs dropped on Japan. In February 1945, 1,400 British planes dropped incendiary bombs on the German city of Dresden. Dresden was packed with refugees and no one knows how many people were in the city. Estimates of the dead in the firestorm range from 250,000 to 500,000.

On March 10, 334 American B-29 bombers firebombed Tokyo, Japan's capital. In one night, 100,000 people died. In comparison, the Hiroshima bomb killed some 70,000 outright with radiation sickness and other injuries bringing the total to 140,000 by the end of the year. At Nagasaki, some 40,000 died outright with 70,000 dead by the end of 1945.

The dropping of the bombs came after years of bloody fighting. Every battle of the war in the Pacific led to higher Allied casualties than predicted. Japanese propaganda portrayed

American marines as monsters who would torture captured
Japanese. Japanese troops and civilians fought to the death on
island after island. At Saipan, a western Pacific island occupied
by Japan at the time of World War II, in 1944, only 2,000 of
27,000 Japanese troops let themselves be taken alive. More
than 20,000 civilians died rather than surrender. Twenty-five
percent of the American troops who attacked Saipan were killed
or wounded.

At Iwo Jima in February 1945, 21,000 Japanese troops
fought 60,000 Americans. Only 212 Japanese troops surren-
dered. The marines' casualty rate was nearly 50 percent (the
highest in the history of the Marine Corps). Thousands of
Japanese civilians leapt to their deaths from high cliffs.

American leaders expected the Japanese to defend their
home islands as vigorously as they had defended the Pacific
islands. The War Department estimated that up to 5 million
Japanese troops defended Japan and predicted that up to 1
million Americans would be killed or wounded in an invasion.
It was thought that more than a million Japanese soldiers
and civilians could die.

The following selection is from a report on President
Harry S. Truman's decision to use the bombs that was prepared by White House press aide Eben A. Ayers. Although
the report is not dated, it was written before President
Truman left office in 1953.

———□———

The Atomic Bomb

On April 25, 1945, Secretary of War Henry L. Stimson had
an appointment with the President at the White House.

Stimson later, in his book "On Active Service In Peace And War" wrote:

> "When Stimson went to the White House on April 25, 1945, to discuss the atomic bomb with a President from whom hitherto the matter had been kept secret, he took with him a memorandum which dealt not so much with the military use of the bomb as with its long-range political meaning."

In his book Stimson quoted the memorandum as follows:

1. Within four months we shall in all probability have completed the most terrible weapon ever known in human history, one bomb of which could destroy a whole city.

2. Although we have shared its development with the U.K., physically the U.S. is at present in the position of controlling the resources with which to construct and use it and no other nation could reach this position for some years.

3. Nevertheless it is practically certain that we could not remain in this position indefinitely. [Editor's note: Stimson discussed the inevitability that other nations would soon develop atomic weapons and the dangers this would create.]

5. The world in its present state of moral advancement compared with its technical development would be eventually at the mercy of such a weapon. In other words, modern civilization might be completely destroyed. [Editor's note: Stimson reported that it would be extremely difficult to

control atomic weapons after the war, even with "such thorough-going rights of inspection and internal controls as we have never heretofore contemplated."]

7. Furthermore, in the light of our present position with reference to this weapon, the question of sharing it with other nations and, if so shared, upon what terms, becomes a primary question of our foreign relations. Also our leadership in the war and in the development of this weapon has placed a certain moral responsibility upon us which we cannot shirk without very serious responsibility for any disaster to civilization which it would further.

8. On the other hand, if the problem of the proper use of this weapon can be solved, we would have the opportunity to bring the world into a pattern in which the peace of the world and our civilization can be saved. . . ." [sic]

In outlining the history of the development of the atomic bomb in his book, Stimson referred to a paper which he published in February, 1947, in Harper's Magazine and he quoted at length from that article.

He said that it was in the Fall of 1941 that the question of atomic energy was first brought directly to his attention. At that time President Roosevelt appointed a committee consisting of Vice President Henry Wallace, General Marshall, Dr. Vannevar Bush, President of Harvard University and himself to advise the President on questions of policy relating to the study of nuclear fission which was then proceeding both in the United States and Great Britain. [Editor's note: Stimson reported that he was "directly responsible to the President" for oversight of the Manhattan Project that developed the bomb.]

He said the policy adopted and steadily pursued by Roosevelt and his advisors was to spare no effort in securing the earliest possible successful development of an atomic weapon. The original experimental achievement of atomic fission, he pointed out, had occurred in Germany in 1938 and it was known that the Germans had continued their experiments. In 1941 and 1942 they were believed to be ahead of us and it was vital that they should not be the first to bring atomic weapons into the field of battle.

"At no time, from 1941 to 1945," Stimson wrote, "did I ever hear it suggested by the President or by any other responsible member of the Government that atomic energy should not be used in the war." He said the entire purpose of the project was production of a military weapon; "on no other ground could the war-time expenditure of so much time and money have been justified." [Editor's note: The report discusses the financing and oversight of the Manhattan Project that developed the atomic bomb.]

In April (1945), Stimson set up a committee, charged with the functions of advising the President on the various questions raised "by our apparently imminent success in developing an atomic weapon." The committee, known as the Manhattan Committee consisted of Stimson as Chairman, . . . [Editor's note: The report lists the members of the committee, including former vice president James F. Byrnes, various officials, and the presidents of the Carnegie Institute of Washington, the Massachusetts Institute of Technology, and Harvard University.]

The committee's work included the drafting of statements issued immediately after the first bombs were dropped, preparation of a bill for domestic control of atomic energy, and recommendations looking toward international control of atomic energy.

On June 1st, this committee recommended that the bomb be used against Japan, without specific warning, as soon as possible and against such a target as to make its devastating strength clear.

Stimson wrote that they could propose no technical demonstration likely to bring an end to the war—"We see no acceptable alternative to direct military use." Stimson said that the conclusions of the committee were similar to his own although he reached his independently and he felt that to extract a genuine surrender from the Japanese Emperor and his military advisors there must be administered a tremendous shock which would carry convincing truth of our power to destroy the Empire. He felt such an effective shock "would save many times the number of lives, both American and Japanese, that it would cost." He set forth an argument in support of his opinion which he said was held not only by himself but by all his senior military advisors.

In July, 1945, although Japan had been seriously weakened, he said there was no indication of any weakening in the determination to fight rather than to accept unconditional surrender. Estimates of the War Department General Staff indicated that the Japanese army had a total strength of about five million men and there was a warm possibility that the Japanese Government might determine upon resistance to the end which would face the Allies with the task of destroying an armed force of five million men and five thousand suicide aircraft. Plans of the armed forces for the defeat of Japan had been prepared without reliance upon the atomic bomb. They included an intensified sea and air blockade, strategic air bombing through the summer and early fall to be followed on November 1st by invasion of the southern island of Kyushu. This to be followed by an invasion of the main island of Honshu in the Spring of 1946. The total United States military and naval force of five million men would be involved. He said they estimated that if we should be forced to carry this plan to a conclusion with major fighting it would not end until the latter part of 1946 at the earliest. With these thoughts in mind he wrote a memorandum for the President on July 2nd. This was prepared after general discussion and agreement with Joseph C. Crew, Acting Secretary of State and Secretary of the Navy Forrestal. He said this was prompted not by the problem of atomic energy but by American desire to achieve a Japanese surrender without invading the home island.

The memorandum was of considerable length and bore the title "Proposed Program For Japan" and did not mention the atomic bomb. It would propose a carefully-timed warning to Japan before any invasion of the Empire was attempted. He said there was much discussion in Washington about the timing of this warning and that the controlling factor in the end was the date set for the Potsdam Conference. He said it was President Truman's decision that such a warning should be issued by the United States and the United Kingdom from this meeting, with the concurrence of the Head of the Chinese Government so that it would be plain that all Japan's enemies were united. This was done in the Potsdam ultimatum of July 26th. On July 28th, the Japanese Premier rejected the ultimatum.

The New Mexico test of the atomic bomb occurred on July 16th while the President was at Potsdam.

He said a list of suggested targets for the atom bomb was made up and he approved four, including the cities Hiroshima and Nagasaki. The former was bombed on August 6th and the latter on August 9th.

TIMELINE

1933 — Adolf Hitler becomes chancellor of
Germany on January 30.
On March 12, the first concentration camp
is opened at Oranienburg outside Berlin.

1939 — The Nazis invade Poland on September 1.
Britain, France, Australia, and New Zealand
declare war on Germany on September 3.

1940 — On May 10, the Nazis invade France, Belgium,
Luxembourg, and the Netherlands; Winston
Churchill becomes the British prime minister.
The Germans bomb Paris; Dunkirk evacuation
ends on June 3.
On July 1, German U-boats attack merchant
ships in the Atlantic.
The German Blitz against England begins on
September 7.

1941 — On June 22, Germany attacks the Soviet Union
as Operation Barbarossa begins.
The Nazi SS Einsatzgruppen begins mass
murder in June.
On December 7, the Japanese bomb Pearl Harbor.

1942 — On January 20, SS leader Heydrich holds the
Wannsee Conference to coordinate the
"Final Solution of the Jewish Question."
In April, Japanese Americans are sent to
relocation centers.
The Battle of Stalingrad begins on
September 13.

1943 ———— From July 9 to July 1, the Allies land in Sicily. On July 25 and July 26, Mussolini is arrested and the Italian Fascist government falls.

1944 ———— Soviet troops advance into Poland on January 6. D-Day landings take place on June 6.

1945 ———— Dresden is destroyed by a firestorm after Allied bombing raids on February 13 and 14. On April 21, the Soviets reach Berlin. On April 30, Adolf Hitler commits suicide. On May 8, V-E (Victory in Europe) Day is celebrated. The United Nations Charter is signed in San Francisco, California, on June 26. The first atomic bomb is dropped, on Hiroshima, Japan, on August 6. Second atomic bomb dropped, on Nagasaki, Japan, August 9. On September 2, the Japanese sign a surrender agreement, and V-J (Victory over Japan) Day is celebrated.

FOR MORE INFORMATION

Web Sites

Due to the changing nature of Internet links, the Rosen Publishing Group, Inc., has developed an online list of Web sites related to the subject of this book. This site is updated regularly. Please use this link to access the list:

http://www.rosenlinks.com/canf/wwtw

FOR FURTHER READING

Alonso, Karen. *Korematsu v. United States: Japanese-American Internment Camps*. Springfield, NJ: Enslow Publishers, Inc., 1998.

Caroll, Bob. *Battles of World War II: The Battle of Stalingrad*, San Diego: Lucent Books, 1997.

Chang, Iris. *The Rape of Nanking: The Forgotten Holocaust of World War II*. New York: Penguin Books, 1998.

Dupuy, R. Ernest, and Trevor N. Dupuy. *The Harper Encyclopedia of Military History: From 3500 B.C. to the Present.* Revised edition. New York: Harper & Row, 1977.

Frankland, Noble, and Christopher Dowling, eds. *Decisive Battles of the Twentieth Century: Land-Air-Sea*. New York: David McKay Company, Inc., 1976.

Goldhagen, Daniel Jonah. *Hitler's Willing Executioners: Ordinary Germans and the Holocaust*. New York: Alfred A. Knopf, 1996.

Harmon, Fred. *Dynamite Cargo: Convoy to Russia*. New York: The Vanguard Press, 1943.

Leckie, Robert. *Helmet for My Pillow*. New York: Random House, 1957.

Rhodes, Richard. *The Making of the Atomic Bomb*. New York: Simon & Schuster, Inc., 1988.

Shirer, William L. *The Rise and Fall of the Third Reich: A History of Nazi Germany*. New York: Simon & Schuster Inc., 1959.

Waln, Nora. *The House of Exile*. Boston: Little, Brown, and Company, 1933.

ANNOTATED BIBLIOGRAPHY

The Ayers Report. The Truman Presidential Museum and Library. Background Folder of the Decision to Drop the Atomic Bomb Study Collection. http://www.trumanlibrary.org/whistlestop/study_collections/bomb/large/background/text/bmb1tx.htm. Retrieved September 3, 2003.

A report on President Harry S. Truman's decision to use the atomic bombs was prepared by White House press aide Eben A. Ayers. While the report is not dated, it was written before President Truman left office in 1953 and drew upon official records and documents.

Byas, Hugh. *Government by Assassination.* First edition. New York: Alfred A. Knopf, 1942.

Excellent book on Japan before the war by the *New York Times* and *London Times* correspondent in Japan.

Carter, Ross S. *Those Devils in Baggy Pants.* New York: Appleton-Century-Crofts, Inc., 1951. (Reprinted in 1996 by Buccaneer Books.)

One of the best World War II memoirs of combat to come out of the war. Carter fought with the 82nd Airborne Division from North Africa to the end of the war in Europe.

"Winston Churchill's speech to the House of Commons after Dunkirk." http://www.winstonchurchill.org. Retrieved July 16, 2003. Original Source: Great Britain, Parliamentary Debates, House of Commons. (Also cited as Hansard, Parliamentary Debates, House of Commons.)

Following the evacuation of British troops from Dunkirk,

Churchill delivered one of his most famous speeches to Parliament and later to the British people. The speech contained a rousing call to resist German attacks: "We shall defend our Island, whatever the cost may be, we shall fight on the beaches, . . . we shall never surrender."

Haggard, Stephen. "I'll Go to Bed at Noon: A Soldier's Letter to His Sons," *The Atlantic Monthly*, December 1940, Vol. 166, No. 6, pp. 665–682. Copyright 1940, *The Atlantic Monthly* Company.

During the 1930s, a large peace movement resisted the re-arming of Europe. When Hitler attacked Poland in 1939 and war began, Stephen Haggard was one of thousands who rushed to enlist in the war effort.

Hillary, Richard. *The Last Enemy: The Memoir of a Spitfire Pilot*. Short Hills, NJ: Burford Books, 1997. Copyright 1942 by Richard Hillary. Copyright ©1997. Burford Books. Reprinted with permission.

Hillary's record of his training as a pilot and his time in combat during the Battle of Britain. Hillary was severely burned when shot down and the last section of the book deals with his slow, painful recovery.

Hitler's Speech to the Commanders Before the German Attack on Poland (Obersalzberg, August 22, 1939). Woodward, E. L., and Rohan Butler, eds. Documents on British Foreign Policy: 1919–1939, Third Series, Volume VII, 1939, No. 314 and Enclosure, Pages 257–260. London, Her Majesty's Stationary Office, 1954. Crown Copyright Reserved.

A week before German troops attacked Poland in 1939, Hitler spoke with his military commanders. An officer who attended the conference gave his record of the speech to an American reporter who passed it on to the British Embassy in Berlin.

Korematsu v. United States. JUSTICE JACKSON, dissenting. http://www.tourolaw.edu/patch/Korematsu/JACKSON.html Retrieved July 12, 2003. Touro Law Center, Touro College Jacob D. Fuchsberg Law Center, Legal Citation: 323 U.S. 214 (1944).

Many of the greatest opinions written by American judges have been dissents from the judgment of the majority of the court. Robert Jackson's opinion in the case involving the internment of Japanese during World War II is such a dissent. Jackson later became America's chief prosecutor at the Nuremberg war crimes trial in Germany.

Lindbergh, Col. Charles A., "A Plea for American Independence." Radio broadcast on the Mutual Network, October 14, 1940. Printed in *Scribner's Commentator*, December 1940, Vol. 9, No. 2, Pages 69–73.

Charles Lindbergh made the first solo, non-stop flight across the Atlantic Ocean in 1927. Lindbergh became a leading figure in the isolationist movement. He traveled to Germany and returned praising Hitler and apparently awed by German power.

Orwell, George. *The Collected Essays, Journals, and Letters of George Orwell: My Country Right or Left, 1940–1943*, Volume 2, first edition, edited by Orwell, Sonia, and Ian Angus. New York: Harcourt, Brace & World, Inc., 1968. pp. 12–14. Copyright ©1968 by Sonia Brownell Orwell and renewed 1996 by Mark Hamilton, reprinted with permission.

George Orwell was one of the most influential critics and
writers of the twentieth century. His insight into Hitler
shows the insight he brought to nearly all of the topics he
wrote about.

Pyle, Ernie. *Brave Men*. New York: Henry Holt and Company,
1944, pp. 440–443. Copyright © 1944. Reprinted with
permission of Scripps Howard Foundation.
Ernie Pyle was a skilled, well-established reporter before
America's involvement in World War II. His reports
focused on the actions of the average soldiers rather than
on the famous generals. Pyle became one of the best
correspondents of the war.

Rhodes, Richard. *Masters of Death: The SS-Einsatzgruppen and the
Invention of the Holocaust*. New York: Alfred A. Knopf, 2002.
Copyright © 2002 by Richard Rhodes. Used by permission of
Alfred A. Knopf, a division of Random House, Inc.
Writer Richard Rhodes is known for meticulous research
and solid writing about complex subjects. His histories
of the atomic bomb (*The Making of the Atomic Bomb*) and
the hydrogen bomb (*Dark Sun: The Making of the
Hydrogen Bomb*) are considered the definitive histories of
both projects.

Ringelblum, Emmanuel. *Notes from the Warsaw Ghetto: The
Journal of Emmanuel Ringelblum*. Edited and translated by
Jacob Sloan. New York: McGraw-Hill Book Company,
Inc., 1958.
Emmanuel Ringelblum led a small group of scribes and
historians who documented the terrors of the Warsaw
Ghetto. His journal is a vital narrative of life under

inhuman conditions. It was smuggled out of the ghetto before the 1943 rising against the Germans. His journal was found in the rubble of Warsaw after the war.

Haile Selassie's Speech to the League of Nations. June 30, 1936, Geneva, Switzerland. http://www.apl.jhu.edu/~yabera/him_geneva.html. The Johns Hopkins University.

Haile Selassie was emperor of Ethiopia in 1935 when more than 300,000 Italian troops invaded. After being forced into exile, Haile Selassie appeared at the League of Nations and told the world of the events of the Italian invasion and warned the nations of Europe that war might come to them next.

Schneider, Franz, and Charles Gullans, trans. *Last Letters from Stalingrad*. New York: William Morrow and Company, 1962. Copyright 1961, The Hudson Review, Inc., pp. 21–22, 32–33, 50–51, 65–66, 83, 91–92. English translation copyright © 1962 by Fran Schneider and Charles Gullans. Reprinted with permission of HarperCollins Publishers, Inc.

In the summer of 1942, the German army attacked southern Russia. Some 300,000 German troops reached Stalingrad but soon became trapped by a Russian counterattack. The letters in this book were written by German soldiers who knew they would soon die or become prisoners of war. The letters were on the last plane the German air force flew out of the city. They were found after the war.

Shirer, William L. *Berlin Diary: The Journal of a Foreign Correspondent, 1934–1941*. First edition. New York: Alfred A. Knopf, 1941, pp. 49–56.

Shirer was a correspondent in Berlin before the war. *Berlin Diary* is his record of events at the time. His post-war book, *The Rise and Fall of the Third Reich: A History of Nazi Germany*, remains the best one-volume history of the Nazi regime.

Smith, Denis Mack. *Mussolini.* New York: Alfred A. Knopf, 1982. The book is an academic, but well-written history of Mussolini by an American historian.

Smith, Howard K. *Last Train from Berlin.* Fifth printing, first edition. New York: Alfred A. Knopf, 1942. Howard K. Smith worked as a reporter for the United Press in Germany in the years before the war. He was the last reporter to leave the country before Germany and the United States declared war on each other in December 1941. He later worked for CBS radio, reporting from England during the war.

Waln, Nora. "Letters from the Manchurian Border," *The Atlantic Monthly.* Part 1, "Under Fire," May 1932. Part 2, "The War that Is Not War," June 1932. A report written by an American woman who lived in China during the years before the start of World War II.

Werner, Herbert A. *Iron Coffins: A Personal Account of the German U-boat Battles of World War II.* First edition. New York: Holt, Rinehart and Winston, 1969. Copyright 1969. One of the best memoirs of the U-boat war, written by one of the few long-service U-boat captains to survive the war.

INDEX

A

appeasement, 7
atomic bomb, 9, 154–155
excerpt from the Ayers Report on the decision to drop the Atomic bomb, 155–161
Ayers, Eben A., 155

B

Babi Yar, 99
Battle of Britain, 130–131
exerpt from *The Last Enemy*, 131–137
Berlin Diary: The Journal of a Foreign Correspondent, 1934–1941, excerpt from, 36–43
Brave Men, excerpt from, 147–153
Byas, Hugh, 28
excerpt from *Government by Assassination,* 28–35

C

Carter, Ross S., 121–122
excerpt from "Those Devils in Baggy Pants," 122–129
Chamberlain, Neville, 7
China
excerpt on Japan's invasion of Manchuria by Nora Waln, 46–53
Japanese invasion of, 6, 7, 8, 44–45
Churchill, Winston, 88, 94–95
"We Shall Fight on the Beaches" speech, 95–97
Communism/Communists, 5, 8, 11, 39, 78
Czechoslovakia, 7

E

Enabling Bill, 19–20

Ethiopia
Haile Selassie's speech to the League of Nations, 54–62
Italian wars in/invasion of, 6, 7, 36, 53–54
Executive Order 9066, 81

F

Fascism/Fascists, 5, 8, 9, 11–12, 28, 53, 80
excerpt from *Mussolini,* 12–19
France
and appeasement, 7
and evacuation of Dunkirk, 94–95
excerpt from *Berlin Diary,* 36–43
and Treaty of Locarno, 35–36
"We Shall Fight on the Beaches" speech by Winston Churchill, 95–97

G

Germany
and the Battle of Britain, 130–131
excerpt from *Berlin Diary,* 36–43
excerpt from *Last Train from Berlin,* 20–27
invasion of Poland, 6, 44, 62, 76, 89, 98, 108
invasion of the Rhineland, 7, 25, 35–36
speech by Adolf Hitler before German attack on Poland, 90–93
in World War I, 11
Government by Assassination, excerpt from, 28–35
Great Britain
and appeasement, 7
and the Battle of Britain, 130–131

and evacuation of Dunkirk,
94–95
exerpt from *The Last Enemy*,
131–137
and Treaty of Locarno, 35–36
"We Shall Fight on the Beaches"
speech by Winston Churchill,
95–97
Guderian, Heinz, 94

H
Haggard, Stephen, 62–63
article/letter to sons, 63–69
Hillary, Richard, 131
excerpt from *The Last Enemy*,
131–137
Himmler, Heinrich, 99
excerpt from *Masters of Death*,
99–107
Hitler, Adolf
and Battle of Britain, 130–131
excerpt from *Berlin Diary*,
36–43
excerpt from *Masters of Death*,
99–107
review of *Mein Kampf* by George
Orwell, 77–81
rise to power, 19–20
speech before German attack on
Poland, 90–93
and Treaty of Locarno, 35–36
Holocaust, 5–6, 99
excerpt from *Masters of Death*,
99–107
excerpt from *Notes from the
Warsaw Ghetto*, 109–115

I
"I'll Go to Bed at Noon: A Soldier's
Letter to His Sons," 63–69
*Iron Coffins: A Personal Account of
the German U-boat Battles of
World War II*, excerpt from,
138–145

Italy
excerpt from *Mussolini*, 12–19
Haile Selassie's speech to the
League of Nations, 54–62
invasion of/wars in Ethiopia, 6,
7, 36, 53–54
in World War I, 11

J
Jackson, Justice Robert, 81
dissenting opinion in *Korematsu
v. United States*, 82–88
Japan
and atomic bomb, 9–10,
154–155, 159–161
attack on Pearl Harbor, 6, 62,
69, 70, 81
excerpt from the Ayers
Report on the decision
to drop the Atomic bomb,
155–161
excerpt from *Government by
Assassination*, 28–35
excerpt on Japan's invasion of
Manchuria by Nora Waln,
46–53
invasions of Manchuria and
China, 6, 7, 8, 28, 44–45
Japanese Americans, 81
dissenting opinion in
Korematsu v. United States,
82–88
Jews/anti-Semitism in World War II,
5, 70, 98–99, 108
excerpt from *Masters of Death*,
99–107
excerpt from *Notes from the
Warsaw Ghetto*, 109–115

K
Korematsu, Fred, 81
Korematsu v. United States dissenting
opinion by Justice Robert
Jackson, 82–88

L

Last Enemy: The Memoir of a Spitfire Pilot, The, excerpt from, 131–137
"Last Letters from Stalingrad," excerpt from, 116–121
Last Train from Berlin, excerpt from, 20–27
League of Nations
    creation of, 7
    speech by Haile Selassie, 54–62
Lindbergh, Charles, 69–70
    radio broadcast, 70–75
Lochner, Louis P., 89
Luftwaffe, 94, 130–131
    excerpt from The Last Enemy, 131–137

M

Manchuria, 6, 7, 28, 44–45
    excerpt on Japan's invasion of Manchuria by Nora Waln, 46–53
Masters of Death: The SS-Einsatzgruppen and the Invention of the Holocaust, excerpt from, 99–107
Mein Kampf, 77
    review by George Orwell, 77–81
Munich Conference, 7
Murphy, Justice Frank, 81
Mussolini, Benito
    excerpt from Mussolini, 12–19
    rise to power, 11–12, 53
Mussolini, excerpt from, 12–19

N

Nazis
    excerpt from Masters of Death, 99–107
    excerpt from Notes from the Warsaw Ghetto, 109–115
    rise to power, 19–20

Notes from the Warsaw Ghetto, excerpt from, 109–115

O

Oppenheimer, Robert, 154
Orwell, George, 76–77
    review of Mein Kampf, 77–81

P

Pearl Harbor, Hawaii, attack on, 6, 62, 69, 70, 81
Perry, Matthew, 27
Poland
    excerpt from Notes from the Warsaw Ghetto, 109–115
    German invasion of, 6, 44, 62, 76, 89, 98, 108
    speech by Adolf Hitler before German attack, 90–93
Pyle, Ernie, 145–147
    excerpt from Brave Men, 147–153

R

Rape of Nanking, 45
Rhineland, German invasion of, 7, 25, 35–36
    excerpt from Berlin Diary, 36–43
Rhodes, Richard, 99
    excerpt from Masters of Death, 99–107
Ringelblum, Emmanuel, 108–109
    excerpt from Notes from the Warsaw Ghetto, 109–115
Roberts, Justice Owen J., 81
Rommel, Erwin, 94
Roosevelt, Franklin D., 81, 157
Royal Air Force, 94, 130–131
    exerpt from The Last Enemy, 131–137
Russo-Japanese War, 44

S

Selassie, Haile, 54

speech to the League of Nations, 54–62
Shinto, 28
  excerpt from *Government by Assassination*, 28–35
Shirer, William L., 36
  excerpt from *Berlin Diary*, 36–43
shoguns, 27
Smith, Denis Mack, excerpt from *Mussolini*, 12–19
Smith, Howard K., 20
  excerpt from *Last Train from Berlin*, 20–27
Socialism/Socialists, 11, 21, 77, 78, 80
Soviet Union/Russia, 8, 9, 36, 39, 76, 90, 91, 92, 93, 98
  Battle of Stalingrad, 115–116
SS Einsatzgruppen, 98–99
  excerpt from *Masters of Death*, 99–107
Stalin, Joseph, 76–77, 80, 90, 91
Stalingrad, 116
  excerpt from "Last Letters from Stalingrad," 116–121

T
"Those Devils in Baggy Pants," excerpt from, 122–129
totalitarianism, 4, 5, 8, 12, 76
Treaty of Locarno, 35–36
  excerpt from *Berlin Diary*, 36–43
Treaty of Versailles, 25, 35, 36, 39
Truman, Harry S., 155
  excerpt from the Ayers Report on the decision to drop the Atomic bomb, 155–161

U
U-boats, 137–138
  excerpt from *Iron Coffins*, 138–145

United States
  attack on Pearl Harbor, 6, 62, 69, 70, 81
  and dropping of atomic bomb, 154–155
  excerpt from the Ayers Report on the decision to drop the Atomic bomb, 155–161
  radio broadcast by Charles Lindbergh, 70–75

W
Waln, Nora, 45
  excerpt on Japan's invasion of Manchuria, 46–53
Warsaw Ghetto, 108–109
  excerpt from *Notes from the Warsaw Ghetto*, 109–115
Werner, Herbert A., 138
  excerpt from *Iron Coffins*, 138–145
"We Shall Fight on the Beaches" speech by Winston Churchill, 95–97
World War I, 4, 6–7, 11, 35

About the Editor

James Fiscus is a Portland, Oregon, writer and historian. He has a master's degree in Middle East and Asian history and taught military history at Portland State University when in graduate school. Before obtaining his MA degree, he worked as a photojournalist in Portland. He served in the U.S. Navy in Vietnam. He has written books on America's war in Afghanistan, the 1956 Suez Crisis in the Middle East, and America's occupation of Iraq. In addition to writing about history, he reports on medicine, science, business, and law for numerous publications.

Credits

Cover © Hulton/Archive/Getty Images, Inc.

Designer: Thomas Forget; Series Editor: Mark Beyer